AF614744

MULTI-AGENT SYSTEMS - CONTROL SPECTRUM

Edited by **Vladimir Shikhin**

Multi-Agent Systems - Control Spectrum
http://dx.doi.org/10.5772/intechopen.75286
Edited by Vladimir Shikhin

Contributors

Héctor Soza, Akinwale Akinwunmi, Emmanuel Olajubu, Ganiyu Aderounmu, Zhong Wang, Yasushi Kambayashi, Munehiro Takimoto, Ryotaro Oikawa, Vladimir Shikhin

Notice

First published in London, United Kingdom, 2019 by IntechOpen
IntechOpen is the global imprint of INTECHOPEN LIMITED, registered in England and Wales, registration number: 11086078, The Shard, 25th floor, 32 London Bridge Street
London, SE19SG – United Kingdom
Printed in Croatia

British Library Cataloguing-in-Publication Data
A catalogue record for this book is available from the British Library

Additional hard copies can be obtained from orders@intechopen.com

Multi-Agent Systems - Control Spectrum, Edited by Vladimir Shikhin
p. cm.
Print ISBN 978-1-78985-751-1
Online ISBN 978-1-78985-752-8

For EU product safety concerns:
IN TECH d.o.o., Prolaz Marije Krucifikse Kozulić 3, 51000 Rijeka, Croatia, info@intechopen.com or visit our website at intechopen.com.

Meet the editor

Vladimir Shikhin received his Engineer Diploma with highest distinction in Automation from Moscow Power Engineering Institute, and his PhD in 1982. He served as Associate Professor until 1994. He was a Post-Doctoral Fellow with the Queen Mary College, University of London in 1985/86. From 1994 to 1999, he was with the Frederick University (Cyprus) as a Professor. From 1999 to 2013, he served in industry. He joined GE RUS in 2009 as the Technical Solutions Director and left in 2013 for the position of Head of the Department of Control & Informatics at the National Research University "MPEI". He is currently a Director of R&D Lab "Energy and technological processes optimization and automation", a member of CIGRE (Russian section) since 2017, and a senior member of IEEE since 1995. His research interests include control systems design and cyber-physical systems analysis.

Contents

Preface

Research in the area of MAS design and control has become very significant in the last few years because of the numerous and undeniable advantages that it introduces in comparison to conventional approaches. This trend follows the need to make control processes more reliable, adjustable, efficient, and flexible under existing systems network topology, as well as to integrate the increasing capabilities of distributed agents. Interconnected agents can be of different nature and have sharply differing features. Accurate study of the agents' destination and behavior, system architecture, links, and interaction processes allow us to find proper mathematical presentation of the systems under study and signal processes flow. The aim of this book is to support further efforts in obtaining new solutions in the area of control design problems with reference to the wide variety of MAS-based approach applications.

Vladimir Shikhin
Department of Control and Informatics
National Research University MPEI
Moscow, Russia

Chapter 1

Introductory Chapter: Major Automatic Control Challenges in Multi-Agent Systems

Vladimir Shikhin

Additional information is available at the end of the chapter

http://dx.doi.org/10.5772/intechopen.83450

This book discusses the multi-agent systems (MAS), which we will consider as intelligent hierarchical distributed dynamic systems that consist of two or more intelligent agents, and each intelligent agent has its separate (local) goals that may match or contradict the goals of other agents. Also, each agent has a certain degree of autonomy.

Until now, there is no general consensus of what is meant by an "agent." However, one of the globally recognized definitions of the "agent" (or "intelligent agent") assumes a computerized system that is situated at some environment and that is capable of autonomous action in this environment in order to meet its objectives.

Based on the previously formulated concept of intelligent agents, we can define their basic properties:

- Active and passive reactivity, $Z(t) = [Z_1(t), Z_2(t),\ldots, Z_g(t)]^T$—vector matrix of the output variables characterizing the flow of physical processes in the system over time for each ith of q agents as a response to a combination of input constraints and set points $U_i(t) = [L_i, D^C_i, D^R_i]^T$, where L_i is the technological limitations of the ith agent, D^C_i is the vector of input commands, and D^R_i is the vector of input recommendations, $i = \overline{1, q}$.
- The ability for goal detection, $Y^{AG} = [Y^{AG}_1, Y^{AG}_2,\ldots,Y^{AG}_e]^T$—vector of objective functions of number l
- Goal-directed behavior, accompanied by the changes in the states of the ith agent $S_i(t)$
- Interaction ability between sending and receiving agents, i.e., senders and receivers, respectively, by exchanging $D_i(t)$ signal, which is perceived by the receiver agent as one of the input vector $D^C(t)$ components

In a multi-agent system, it is necessary to take into account that agents function under the conditions of some environment that may act as a source of measurable and immeasurable noise and disturbances, $V(t) = [v_1(t), v_2(t),\ldots, v_k(t)]^T$—vector of disturbances (immeasurable).

Based on the concept of homogeneous and heterogeneous systems, we will define both types as follows: agents are considered homogeneous if they have the same goals Y, are characterized by identical sets of possible states $S(t)$, and have similar set points and output constraints $Z(t)$. Otherwise, if they differ in one or more of the mentioned factors, the agents are considered heterogeneous.

Figure 1 shows the generalized structure of the MAS, taking into account the interaction of agents.

Recently, the representation of dynamic systems in the form of MAS and the use of appropriate methods for analysis and design are being applied more and more in various fields and applications. For example, we can find its implementation in processing control tasks in robotic systems, in intelligent electrical systems, etc. Although there are many examples in

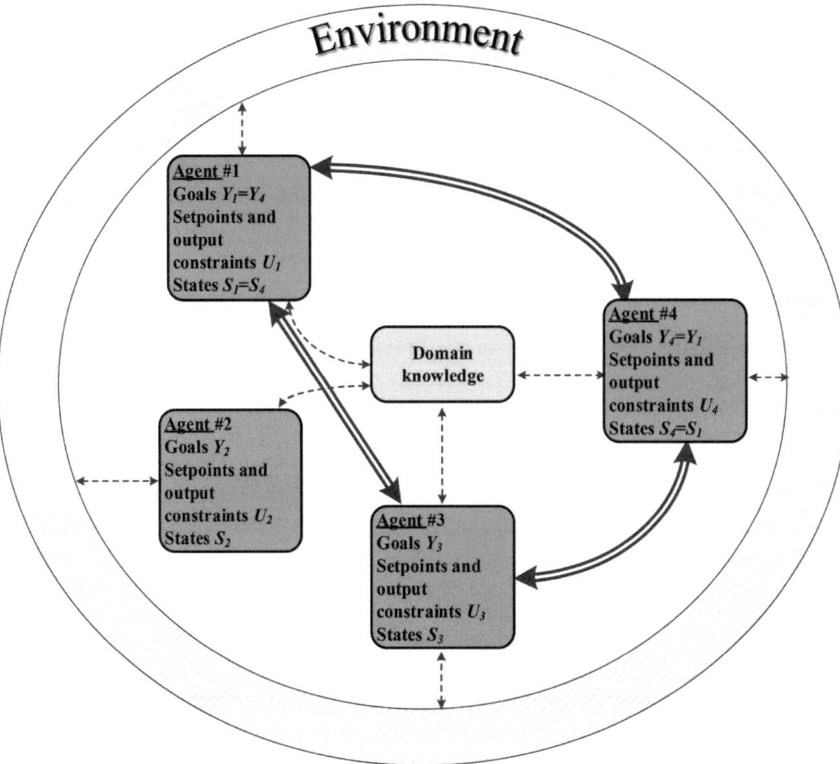

Figure 1. MAS consisting of homogeneous (#1, #4) and heterogeneous agents (#2, #3), communicating (#1, #3, #4) and noncommunicating (#2) agents.

http://dx.doi.org/10.5772/intechopen.83450

the publications related to multi-agent applications, there are some numerical data of practical solutions. This makes it difficult to assess the efficiency of MAS-oriented approaches in comparison with alternative approaches.

Nevertheless, the development of agent-based technologies plays an increasing role in designing cyber-physical systems (CPS), allowing to create decentralized control systems based on the distribution of control functions between autonomous and cooperative agents, realizing such important characteristics as modularity, flexibility, reliability, reconfigurability, etc. Applying multi-agent technologies in the applications to cyber-physical systems leads to development of the new methods to execute control tasks by creating systems with a combined centralized and decentralized control.

Solving problems associated with multiple-criteria control can be associated with multi-agent representation, especially when there exist conflicting criteria and some uneven distributions between heterogeneous subjects of the dynamic system. Such approach introduces efficient methods for dealing with the corresponding optimization problems.

It seems promising to use a MAS-oriented approach to solve the problems associated with multi-purpose control, especially in the presence of conflicting criteria and some uneven distribution of criteria between heterogeneous subjects of the dynamic system.

Despite the existing problems, multi-agent approaches could be considered an effective tool for control and decision-making in systems where there are distributed control and uncertainty related to the control law implemented by each agent, poorly predictable environmental behavior, and possible losses in total observability and controllability of the subjects.

It is known that the solution of control problems in complex dynamic systems, which are usually understood as high-dimensional systems, containing branching and cross-links, and different types of uncertainties, nonlinearities, etc., is associated with approaches based on the decomposition of such systems. In this regard, multi-agent technologies offer particularly such a decomposition, for example, based on the individual and cooperating agents entering into consideration.

Regarding the content of the particular issue, "Multi-Agent Systems: Control Spectrum," it can take several directions of theoretical investigations and different practical areas for applications as it follows from the variety of the presented chapters.

Author details

Vladimir Shikhin

Address all correspondence to: shikhinva@mpei.ru

Department of Control and Informatics, National Research University MPEI, Moscow, Russia

Chapter 2

Quality Measures for Agent-Oriented Software

Héctor Soza

Additional information is available at the end of the chapter

http://dx.doi.org/10.5772/intechopen.79741

Abstract

The popularity of software agents and multiagent systems has increased, and this is now one of the most active areas in informatics research and development. Agent-oriented software engineering is a new paradigm. But no paradigm would be complete without a means for measuring its quality. This work is the result of an investigation in order to evaluate characteristics of a software agent, measuring its most relevant characteristics. For this, we consider the three most important characteristics of a software agent: its social ability, autonomy and proactivity. Measurable attributes are defined for each feature and then are defined measures to evaluate each attribute, and from these values obtain the value of the characteristics considered are proposed. To validate these measures are applied to a case study.

Keywords: agent quality, social ability, proactivity, autonomy, software quality

1. Introduction

Software quality has been a major issue in software development history. The ultimate aim is to ensure user satisfaction with the reliability and operation of software products based on well-defined characteristics. Several software quality models have been produced, such as the procedural model [1], the object-oriented model [2] and the international standard quality model established by ISO and IEC [3].

To evaluate the software agent, published works have been investigated in relation to measures to evaluate it, which mainly consider the adoption of measures of other paradigms, such as procedural and object-oriented, since there are programming characteristics in common with software oriented to agents, such as modular programming and encapsulation [4, 5].

We are interested in applying the software quality model for another type of software: agent systems. We take the viewpoint that it is essential to analyze the key software agent characteristics in order to evaluate the quality of a software agent. These characteristics define agent behavior inside a multi-agent system and include social ability, autonomy, proactivity, reactivity, adaptability, intelligence and mobility [6, 7].

In this chapter, we present the study of the characteristics of social ability, autonomy and proactivity, with their attributes and associated measures, considering that they are the most representative of the software agent [8–10]. The objective of this research work is to propose attributes associated with these characteristics of the software agent and a set of measures that allow evaluating these attributes [11].

To evaluate the quality of software, ISO/IEC proposed in 2001 to decompose this quality into three hierarchical levels: characteristics (correspond to properties that the software must verify), sub-characteristics or attributes (they are measurable qualities that influence each characteristic) and measurements (are the metrics that allow evaluating the attributes) [3]. Based on this decomposition, this research work has been proposed to evaluate the characteristics of a software agent.

The rest of the chapter is structured as follows. The characteristic of an agent is defined, and attributes related to social ability, autonomy and proactivity are presented. Then, works related to the development of measures to evaluate characteristics of the software agent are presented. Next, measures to evaluate the attributes associated with these characteristics are described, and their application to a case study is presented. The chapter ends with a series of conclusions and lines of future research.

2. Characteristics of the agent software

According to McCall [1] and ISO/IEC [3], to measure the quality of a software product, three aspects of the product must be defined: its characteristics, its sub-characteristics (called attributes) and the measurements of these attributes.

The characteristics considered in this work as more representative of a software agent are its social ability, autonomy and proactivity [11]. **Table 1** summarizes these characteristics, providing a short definition and a list of relevant attributes that we identified in [11].

The importance of the social ability is that in order to achieve its objectives, the agent must be able to communicate, negotiate and cooperate with the other agents of the system [6, 11].

The importance of autonomy lies in the fact that in order to achieve an objective the agent must have the possibility to decide, not only how to achieve an objective, but also that the objectives must be sought on the basis of an interest generated endogenously [12], must control their internal state, have independence and the ability to adapt to the needs of their environment [10].

Characteristics	Definition	Attributes
Social ability	The agent is able to interact with other agents, and possibly humans, in order to achieve its design objectives.	• Communication • Cooperation • Negotiation
Autonomy	The agent is able to operate on its own without the need for any human guidance or the intervention of external elements. It has control over its own actions and internal states.	• Self-control • Encapsulation • Learning • Evolution
Proactivity	The agent is able to exhibit goal-directed behavior by taking the initiative in order to achieve its design objectives. This capability often requires the agent to anticipate future situations (to take the initiative), to interact with other agents and to perceive its environment.	• Initiative • Interaction • Reaction

Table 1. Characteristics and attributes of software agents.

The importance of proactivity is that it implies that the agent executes actions on his own initiative to achieve his objectives, interacting with the agents in the environment and reacting to the stimuli that appear in this environment, so he must have the ability to evaluate their environment and decide what action to take [13, 14].

3. Related work

Considering the research developed on the characteristics and quality measures of a software agent, until before 2013, few studies in the literature had focused on proposing measures related to the characteristics of social ability, autonomy and proactivity of a software agent and few specify a set of specific measures to evaluate these characteristics.

In [4], it is proposed to measure the social ability of the agent using the complexity of the agent as a way of knowing the degree of the organizational dimensions of the agent (such as social, relational, environmental and personal).

Cernuzzi and Rossi proposed a framework for an evaluation of the analysis and design of agent-oriented modeling methods. They evaluate the autonomy of an agent considering whether or not the modeling techniques check whether the agents have control over their internal state and behavior [15].

In 2004, Shin presented the results of adapting some measures of procedural and object-oriented paradigms to agent-oriented software, as well as adding specific measures for this paradigm. In his work, he does not define attributes to evaluate these characteristics; he only defines measures to assess some aspects of these characteristics of the agent's software [16].

Huber proposes measuring social dependence to evaluate autonomy. To calculate a global value of the autonomy of a software agent, Huber combines the value of the autonomy of social integrity and the value of the autonomy of the dependency [17].

The state of the art revealed the need to propose measures that would allow evaluating the most relevant characteristics of the software agent, with appropriate measures that consider the attributes related to these characteristics.

4. Attributes and measures

The measures proposed for each attribute are the result of research in software agents. Some were selected from the procedural and object-oriented paradigms, and others are new measures specially designed to evaluate these attributes [11].

4.1. Attributes and measures of social ability

The social ability in the agents is the competence they have at the moment of exchanging information between them (communication), the ability in the joint collaboration (cooperation) and the ability to reach an agreement on the way forward to reach their objectives (negotiation) [18].

The communication attribute is identified with the agent's ability to receive and send messages by the agent to achieve its objectives. It has been determined that a good communication of the agent can be evaluated considering: the number of messages invoked in response to a message received by the agent (RFM), the size of the messages sent by the agent during execution (AMS), and the number of incoming and outgoing messages received (FIM) and sent (FOM) by the agent to maintain a significant communication link or perform some objectives [16, 18].

The cooperation attribute is identified with the agent's ability to respond to the services requested by other agents and offer services to other agents. It has been determined that good cooperation can be evaluated considering: the agent's ability to accept or reject services requested by other agents (SRRA), and the agent's ability to offer services (ASA) [6, 18].

The negotiation attribute is identified with the agent's ability to establish commitments, resolve conflicts and reach agreements with other agents to ensure compliance with its objectives. Therefore, this attribute can be evaluated considering: the number of objectives achieved (AGA), the number of messages sent by the agent when another agent requires a service from it (MRS), and the number of messages sent by the agent when requesting a service from other agents (MSS) [6, 18]. **Table 2** presents the nine proposed measures for evaluating a software agent's social ability and its definitions.

4.2. Attributes and measures of autonomy

Autonomy in agents is understood as the agent's ability to control his own actions (self-control), the ability to manage his behavior and other information related to his actions (functional independence) and the ability to self-adjust and adapt to new requirements (capacity for evolution) [13].

Measures to evaluate the attributes of social ability		
Communication	Answers by message	RFM: Measures the number of messages that are sent in response to a message received by the agent
	Average message size	AMS: Measures the data size of the messages sent by the agent in their communication
	Number of messagesreceived	FIM: Measures the number of messages received in the agent's communication during its lifetime
	Number of messages sent	FOM: Measures the number of messages sent by the agent in the agent's communication during its execution time
Cooperation	Service requests rejected by the Agent	SRRA: Measures the percentage of services rejected by the agent when other agents require their services
	Amount of services offered by the agent	ASA: Measures the amount of services that the agent advertises in the yellow pages directory of their environment
Negotiation	Objectives achieved by the agent	AGA: Measures the efficiency of agent negotiation to achieve its objectives, with the support of other agents in the environment
	Messages for a requested service	MRS: Measures the number of messages exchanged by the agent when conducting a negotiation, when another agent is requesting their services
	Messages sent to request a service	MSS: Measures the number of messages exchanged by the agent when performing a negotiation when the agent requests a service from another agent

Table 2. Measures to evaluate the attributes of social ability.

The self-control attribute is identified with the fact that the agent is able to operate on its own, without the need for human support or the intervention of external elements, to achieve its objectives [13], and with the level of control that the agent has about its own state and behavior [4]. It has been determined that a good self-control of the agent can be evaluated considering: the amount and complexity of the pointers or references that the agent uses in its programming in the agent's internal state (SC), the size of the agent's internal state (ISS), and the complexity of the services that the agent offers (BC) [13].

The functional independence attribute is identified with the executive tasks that require an action that the agent must perform on behalf of any of the users it represents or of other agents [6, 16]. A good level of functional independence indicates that the agent does not have to perform many executive tasks, which can be evaluated considering the fraction of messages requiring action by the user or other agents of the system with respect to all messages received [13]. It has been determined that a good functional independence of the agent can be evaluated considering the influence on the agent of the fraction of executive messages (that request an action) received from the user, to whom the agent represents, or from other agents (to whom it is obligated to respond) with respect to all received messages (EMR) [13].

The attribute capacity of evolution is identified with the agent's ability to adapt to the needs of the environment [19] and take the necessary measures to self-adjust to new objectives [20]. A good capacity for evolution can be evaluated considering: the ability to update its status by the agent (SUC), and the frequency of updating its status (FSU) [13]. **Table 3** presents the six measures proposed to evaluate the agent's autonomy and its definitions.

Measures to evaluate the attributes of autonomy		
Self-control	Structural complexity	SC: Measures the amount and complexity of the pointers or references that the agent uses in its programming in the agent's internal state
	Size of the internal state	ISS: Measures the size of the agent's internal state
	Behavior complexity	BC: Measures the complexity of the services that the agent offers (only applies to agents that offer services)
Functional independence	Fraction of executive type messages	EMR: Measures the influence on the agent of the fraction of executive messages (that request an action) received from the user, to whom the agent represents, or from other agents (to whom it is obligated to respond) with respect to all received messages (considering communication actions)
Capacity of evolution	Capacity to update the status	SUC: Measures the agent's capacity to update its status
	Status update frequency	FSU: Measures the update frequency of the agent's state during execution

Table 3. Measures to evaluate the attributes of autonomy.

4.3. Attributes and measures of proactivity

Proactivity refers to the ability of agents to achieve their goals. To do this, it must make decisions dynamically (initiative), have the ability to relate to obtain information that helps solve problems (interaction) and must act actively in response to environmental stimuli (reaction) [10].

The initiative attribute is identified with the agent's capacity to meet the objectives defined in its design, through goal-directed behavior [6], and to undertake an action on its own with the goal of achieving its objectives [10, 21]. A good initiative capacity can be evaluated considering: the number of roles that the agent must develop (NOR), the number of objectives reached by the agent (AGA), and the average number of messages exchanged by the agent to achieve its objectives (MAG) [10].

The interaction attribute is identified with the agent's capacity to interact with other agents and their environment [10, 22]. A good interaction capacity can be evaluated considering: the number of services implemented within the agent that enable it to achieve its goals (SA), the number of different types of agent messages that the agent can process (NMT) and the average number of public services called per agent (NSC) [10].

The reaction attribute is identified with the agent's capacity to react to a stimulus from the environment according to a stimulus/response behavior [23]. It has been determined that a good capacity for reaction can be evaluated considering: the number of requests received and resolved at runtime (NPR), and the agent's operation complexity (AOC) [10]. **Table 4** presents the eight proposed measures to evaluate the proactivity of a software agent and their definitions.

Figure 1 shows a summary of the characteristics, attributes and measures proposed for the software agent.

Measures to evaluate the attributes of proactivity		
Initiative	Number of roles	NOR: Measures the influence on initiative by the number of roles assigned to an agent in the system under evaluation and defined in the design phase
	Number of goals	AGA: Measures the relationship between the number of goals achieved by the agent during execution over the originally assigned goals
	Messages to achieve goals	MAG: Measures the number of executive messages used to communicate with other system agents to achieve its goals
Interaction	Services per agent	SA: Measures the number of services implemented within the agent (number of implemented public methods or offered services, not including internal methods) that enable it to achieve its goals
	Number of message types	NMT: Measures the number of different types of agent messages that the agent can process
	Number of services called per agent	NSC: Measures the average number of public services called per agent
Reaction	Number of processed requests	NPR: Measures the number of requests received and resolved at runtime
	Agent operations complexity	AOC: Measures the mean complexity of the operations to be performed by the agent to achieve its goals

Table 4. Measures to evaluate the attributes of proactivity.

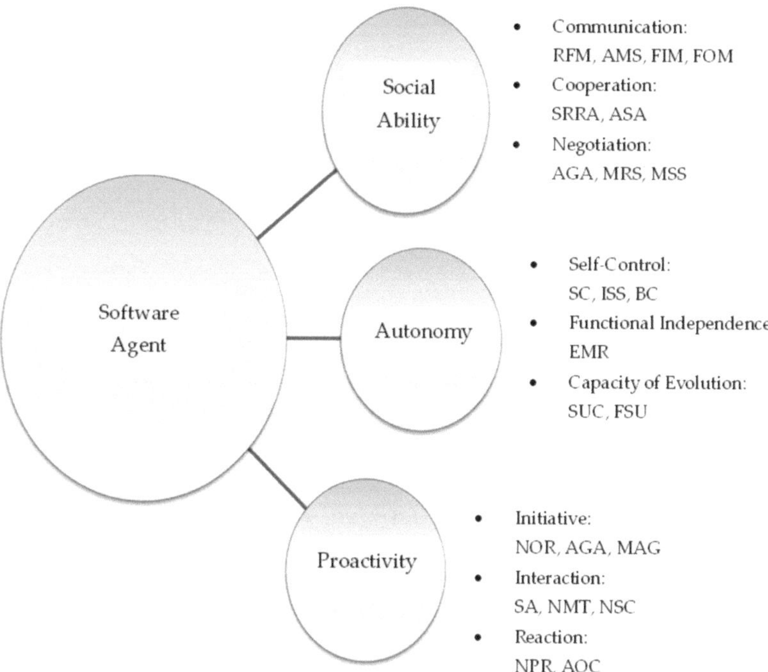

Figure 1. Characteristics, attributes and measures of a software agent.

To use the quality measures, it is proposed to follow the following steps, which are an adaptation of those proposed in [24].

- Determine the weights of the different characteristics, attributes and measures. To do this, the Hierarchical Analysis Method [25] can be used to obtain the relevant matrices adapted to the problem's environment:

  1. The weights of the characteristics are determined from the relevance matrix obtained through surveys to software engineers.
  2. The weights of the attributes for each characteristic are determined, using surveys to the software engineers to determine the matrices of relevance.
  3. The weights of each measure are determined for each attribute.

- Evaluate the values of each measure:

  1. Calculate the values of each measure according to the scope of application
  2. Normalize the proposed measures if necessary

- Based on the weights and the values of the measurements, the following are determined:

  1. The quality values of the attributes of each characteristic
  2. The quality values of each characteristic
  3. The quality value associated with the software agent system

- Analyze the results

5. Study case

Next, a case study corresponding to the agent management process of a banking environment is presented, which considers agents of the bank type, the client type and the facilitator agent, and which performs an exchange of knowledge and actions among these agents (**Figure 2**).

The agents of the system are related through operations typical of a bank, such as creating an account, turning money or requesting a loan. The system consists of two agents of type clients and three agents of type bank, in addition to a facilitator agent. The first one will initiate the conversations and the banks will try to answer them by carrying out internal processes or questions to other entities of the same nature.

To carry out this study, software was used that applied the evaluations of the measures of this work [26, 27].

The JADE platform was used to design the software [28], and the coding was performed in the Eclipse integrated development environment [29]. Three different experiments were carried out to evaluate the different measures exposed in this work. An aspect of the graphical interface of the systems implemented for the banking system is presented in **Figure 3**.

In all the experiments, the opinion of several experts in the development of software oriented to agents with a score between 0 and 10 of the measures considered in the system was considered; and then the Kolmogorov-Smirnov test was applied [30], in which the arithmetic mean of the opinions of the experts and the arithmetic mean of the measures to make them comparable were considered.

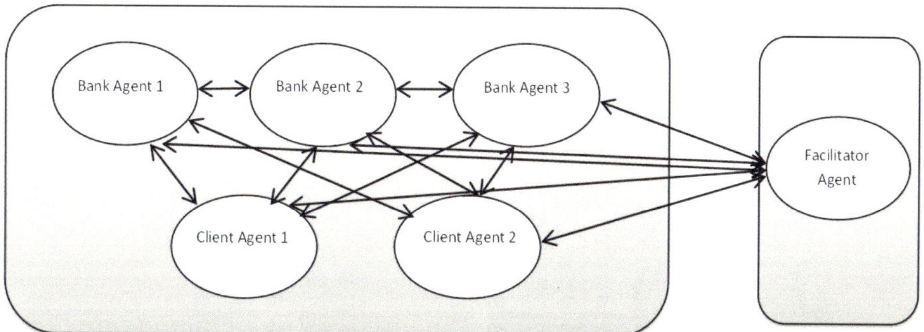

Figure 2. Bank system agents.

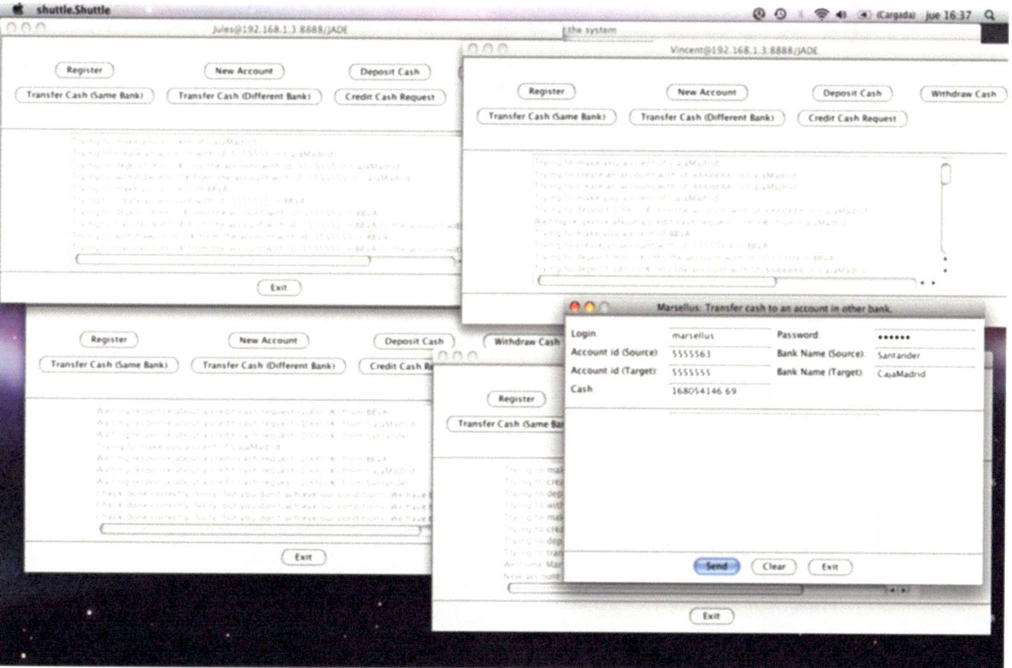

Figure 3. Graphical interface of the banking multi-agent system.

In the first experiment, measures were applied to evaluate the social ability of each agent in the system. **Figure 4** shows the average results for each measure for each attribute and for each agent present in the system. **Figure 5** presents the value of the attributes and the social ability, calculated considering the arithmetic mean of the measurements for each attribute. It is observed that the banking agents have a greater value of the cooperation attribute, while the client agents have it in the negotiation. Analyzing the values for the system, the average values of all the attributes are very similar (around 86%). Finally, the value of the social ability of the system is 86%, which is high for this system.

Regarding the evaluation of experts on the measures of social ability applying the Kolmogorov-Smirnov test, the arithmetic mean of the opinions of the experts and the arithmetic mean of the measurements were taken, obtaining a level of significance of 0.50 that allows to reject the hypothesis that both samples come from different distributions. **Figure 6** presents a comparison of the results of the average obtained by the system and the experts, applying the Kolmogorov-Smirnov test.

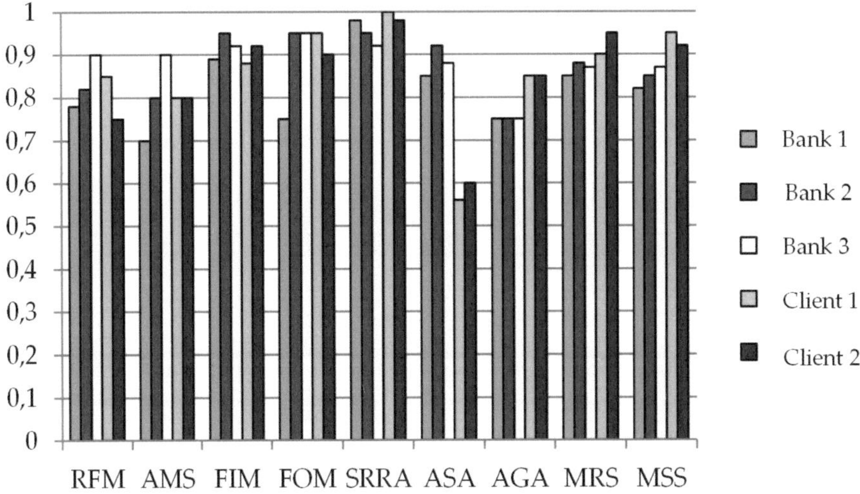

Figure 4. Average values of the measures of the attributes of social ability per agent.

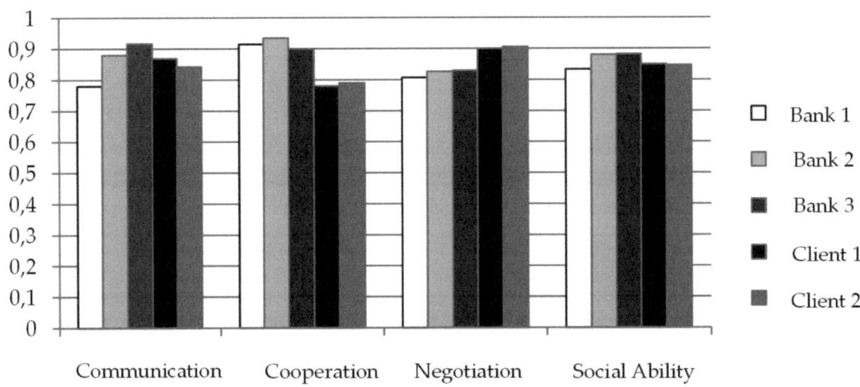

Figure 5. Average values of social ability measures per agent.

In the second experiment, measures were applied to evaluate the autonomy of each agent in the system. **Figure 7** shows the average results for each measure for each attribute and for each agent present in the system. **Figure 8** presents the value of attributes and autonomy, calculated considering the arithmetic mean of the measurements for each attribute. The attributes influence the autonomy value of each agent, being lower than those of the banking agents and a little greater than the one of the client agents because the banking agents have greater capacity of evolution and functional independence. The average autonomy is 80%.

Figure 9 shows the comparison of the results of the average obtained by the system and the experts, applying the Kolmogorov-Smirnov test. Regarding the evaluation of experts on the measures of autonomy of the agents of the system, the arithmetic mean of the opinions of the experts and the arithmetic mean of the measures were considered, obtaining a level of significance of 0.75, which allows to reject the hypothesis that both samples come from different distributions.

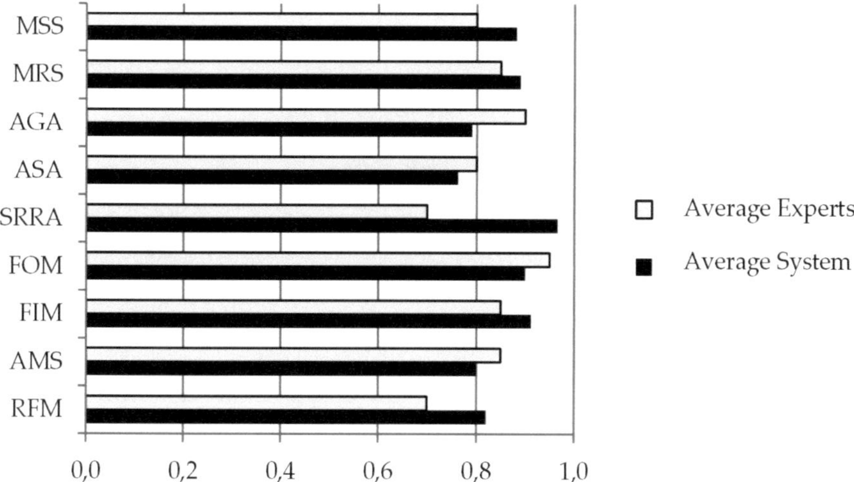

Figure 6. Average values of the experts and the system.

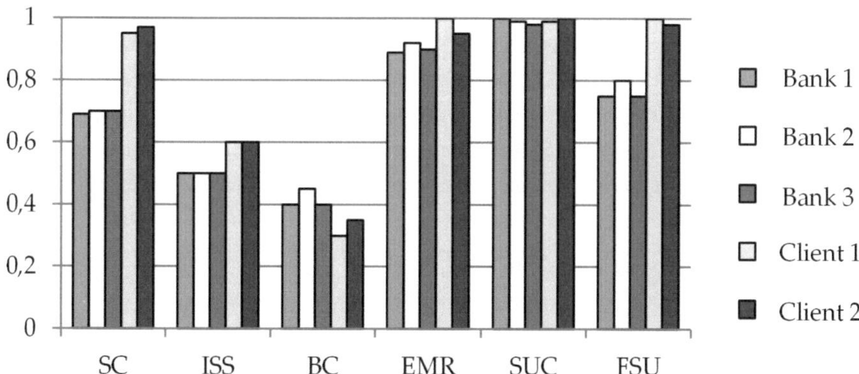

Figure 7. Average values of the measures of the attributes of the autonomy per agent.

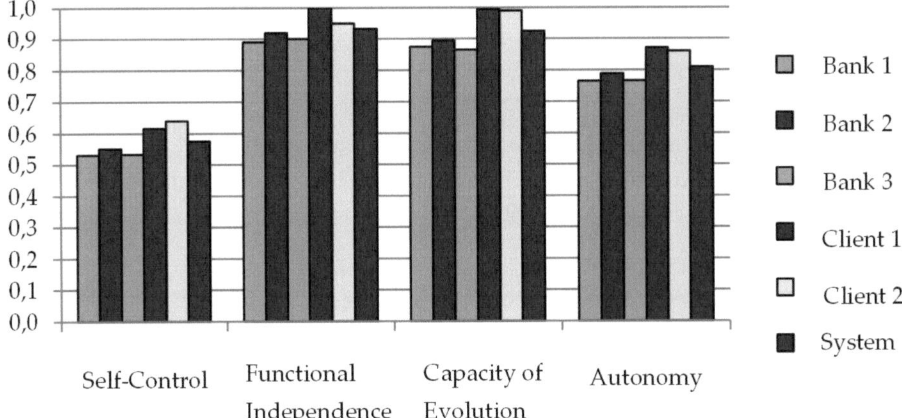

Figure 8. Average values of autonomy measures per agent.

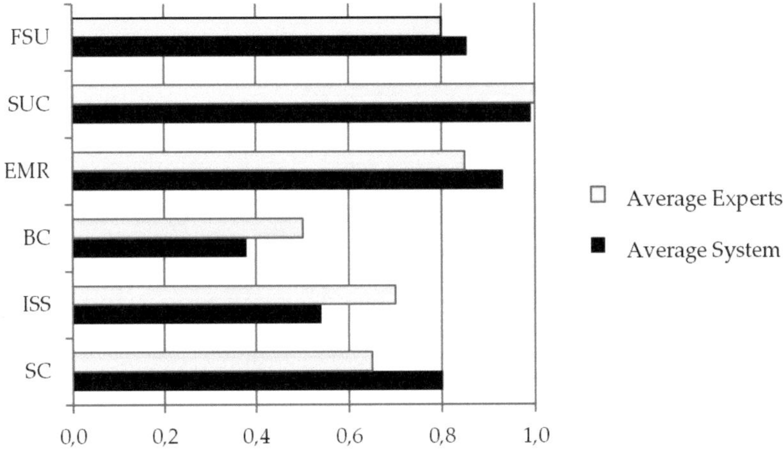

Figure 9. Average values of the experts and the system.

In the third experiment, measures were applied to evaluate the proactivity of each agent in the system. **Figure 10** shows the average results for each measure for each attribute and for each agent present in the system. **Figure 11** shows the value of the attributes and proactivity calculated considering the arithmetic mean of the measurements for each attribute. There are high values of initiative of the banking agents (on average it is 97%) followed by the other two attributes: interaction and reaction (95% on average). Finally, the proactivity of the system of the system is very high, with 96% on average, which is explained by the high interaction of the agents of the system.

Figure 12 shows the comparison of the results of the average obtained by the system and the experts, applying the Kolmogorov-Smirnov test. Regarding the evaluation of experts on the measures of proactivity of the agents of the system, the arithmetic mean of the opinions of the experts and the arithmetic mean of the measures were considered, obtaining a level of significance of 0.45, which allows to reject the hypothesis that both samples come from different distributions.

http://dx.doi.org/10.5772/intechopen.79741

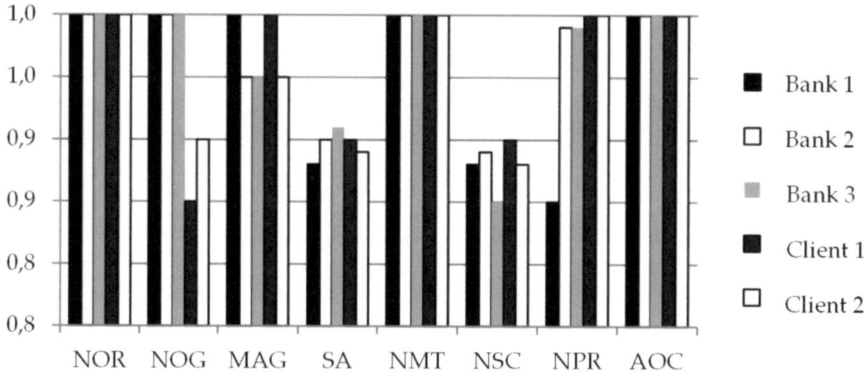

Figure 10. Average values of the measures of the attributes of the proactivity per agent.

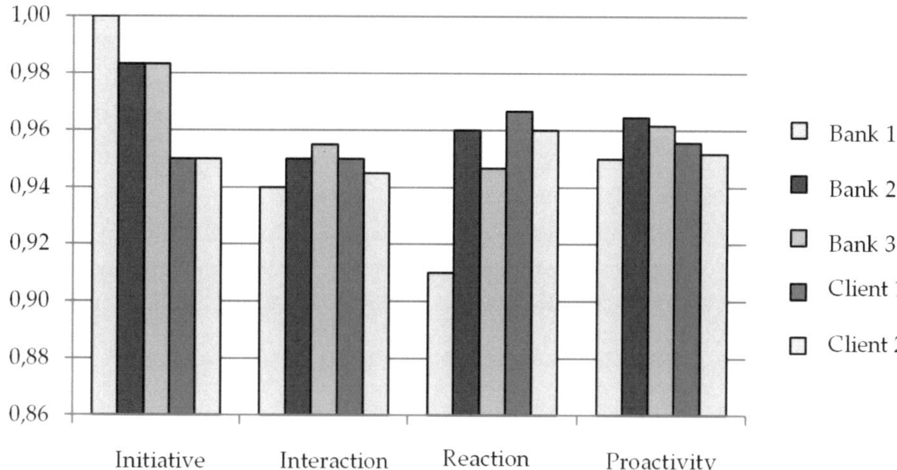

Figure 11. Average values of proactivity measures per agent.

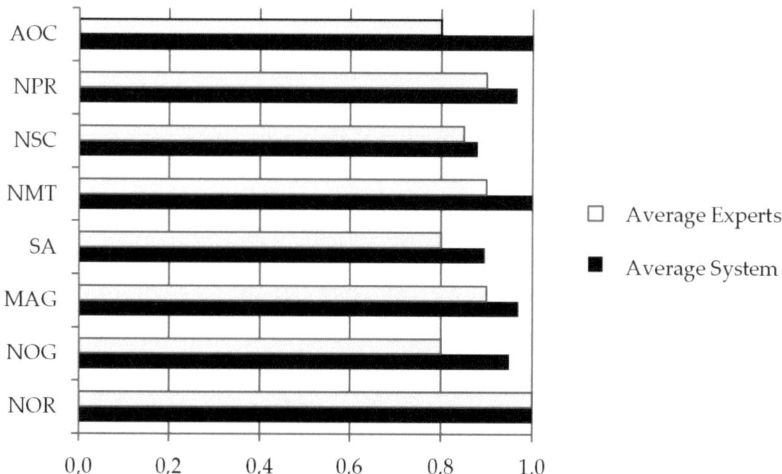

Figure 12. Average values of the experts and the system.

6. Conclusions

From the study of software agent technology, different characteristics present in this type of software were defined. Considering these characteristics, the work of studying three of them was addressed: social ability, autonomy and proactivity. These, in turn, were divided into nine attributes (three for each characteristic), to consider different factors that represent important aspects of each characteristic, susceptible to being evaluated.

For these attributes, 23 measures were designed for the evaluation of these attributes, and they can be used in an agent-oriented application to obtain a consistent evaluation of the characteristics studied.

An application was also developed [26, 27], making use of the Eclipse platform [29] and object orientation in Java, which allowed to implement a form of automatic evaluation of the proposed measures in this work, on different agent-oriented applications, and that shows that the measures developed are automatable. The use of this tool also provided the possibility of refining the measures to study its behavior in greater detail. In addition, the application allowed to modify the values of the weights associated with the measures to determine the most appropriate for each situation under study.

This work constitutes an advance of the research carried out to reach a quality model in the agent-oriented paradigm, which allows developers to have help with which to satisfactorily evaluate their work, in order to ensure that it is appropriate for the functions for which it was produced, considering the characteristics that each component of the application must fulfill.

Author details

Héctor Soza

Address all correspondence to: hsoza@ucn.cl

School of Engineering, Catholic University of the North, Coquimbo, Chile

References

[1] McCall JA. An introduction to software quality metrics. In: Cooper JD, Fisher MJ, editors. Software Quality Management. New York: Petrocelli Books; 2009

[2] Fuertes JL. Modelo de Calidad para el Software Orientado a Objetos. In: [PhD Thesis]. Facultad de Informática. Madrid: Universidad Politécnica de Madrid; 2003

[3] ISO/IEC 9126-1:2001 Software Engineering-Product Quality–Part 1: Quality Model. International Organization for Standardization; 2001

[4] Dumke R, Koeppe R, Wille C. Software Agent Measurement and Self-Measuring Agent-Based Systems. In: Fakultät für Informatik. Otto-von-Guericke-Universität; 2000

[5] Far B, Wanyama T. Metrics for agent-based software development. Proceedings of the IEEE Canadian Conference on Electrical and Computer Engineering. CCECE 2003. pp. 1297-1300

[6] Wooldridge M. An Introduction to Multiagent Systems. Chichester: John Wiley Ltd. Ltd; 2002

[7] Mas A. Agentes Software y Sistemas Multi-Agente: Conceptos, Arquitecturas y Aplicaciones. Madrid: Pearson Educación; 2005

[8] Wooldridge M, Jennings N. Intelligent agents: Theory and practice. The Knowledge Engineering Review. 1995;**10**(2):115-152

[9] Duncan I, Storer T. Agent testing in an ambient world. Proceedings of the Pervasive 2006 Workshop, Dublin, Eire. May, 2006. pp. 757-764

[10] Alonso F, Fuertes JL, Martínez L, Soza H. Measuring the pro-activity of software agents. In: Proceedings of the Fifth International Conference on Software Engineering Advances (ICSEA 2010). France: Nice; August 2010. pp. 319-324

[11] Soza H. Medidas de Calidad para Software Orientado a Agentes. In: Tesis para optar al grado de doctor. Facultad de Informática. Madrid, España: Universidad Politécnica de Madrid; 2013

[12] Bonifacio M, Bouquet P, Ferrario R, Ponte D. Towards a model of goal autonomous agents. Proceedings of the Fourth International Bi-Conference Workshop on Agent-Oriented Information Systems. AOIS '02, 59, pp. 27-28. 2002

[13] Alonso F, Fuertes JL, Martínez L, Soza H. Towards a set of measures for evaluating software agent autonomy. Proceedings of the 8th Mexican International Conference on Artificial Intelligence (MICAI 2009). Guanajuato, México. 2009. pp. 73-78

[14] Chao K-M, James A, Norman P. A framework for intelligent agents within effective concurrent design. Proceedings of the sixth international conference on computer supported cooperative work in design. IEEE. 2001. pp. 338-341

[15] Cernuzzi L, Rossi G. On the evaluation of agent oriented methodologies. Proceedings of the OOPSLA 02 - Workshop on Agent-Oriented Methodologies, Seattle, USA. November, 2002. pp. 21-30

[16] Shin K. Software agents metrics. A preliminary study and development of a metric analyzer. In: Project Report N° H98010. Dept. Computer Science. School of Computing. National University of Singapore; 2003/2004

[17] Huber M. Agent autonomy: Social integrity and social independence. Proceedings of the International Conference on Information Technology ITNG'07, Las Vegas, Nevada. IEEE Computer Society, Los Alamitos, CA, USA. 2007. pp. 282-290

[18] Alonso F, Fuertes JL, Martínez L, Soza H. Measuring the social ability of software agents. Proceedings of the 6th ACIS International Conference on Software Engineering. Research, Management & Applications (SERA 2008). IEEE Computer Society. August, 2008. pp. 3-10

[19] Murdock J. Model-based reflection for agent evolution. In: Technical Report GIT-CC-00-34. Doctoral Thesis. Atlanta: Georgia Institute of Technology; 2000

[20] Friedman B, Nissenbaum H. Software agents and user autonomy. Proceedings of the First International Conference on Autonomous Agents, 1997. pp. 466-469

[21] Rousseau D, Moulin B. Mixed initiative in interactions between software agents. In: Proceedings of the 1997 Spring Symposium on Computer Models for Mixed Initiative Interaction. Portland, Oregon, USA: AAAI Press; March, 1997

[22] Covey S. The Seven Habits of Highly Effective People. London: Simon & Schuster UK Ltd; 1989

[23] Orro A, Saba M, Vargiu E. Using a personalized, adaptive and cooperative multi agent system to predict protein secondary structure. Proceedings of the First International Workshop on Multi-Agent Systems for Medicine, Computational Biology, and Bioinformatics, BIOMED'05, Utrecht, The Netherlands, pp. 170-183. 2005

[24] Fuertes JL. Modelo de Calidad para el Software Orientado a Objetos. In: Tesis para optar al grado de doctor. Facultad de Informática. Madrid, España: Universidad Politécnica de Madrid; 2003

[25] Saaty T. How to make a decision: The analytic hierarchy process. European Journal of Operational Research. 1990;**48**:9-26

[26] Villasante O. Evaluación de Calidad de Sistemas Multiagente: una aplicación práctica a un sistema bancario. In: Memoria de Ingeniero Informático, Facultad de Informática. Universidad Politécnica de Madrid; 2011

[27] Villasante O. Evaluación de Calidad de Sistemas Multi-Agente para entornos JADE. In: Tesis de Master en Informática, Facultad de Informática. Universidad Politécnica de Madrid; 2011

[28] Bellifemine F, Poggi A, Rimassa G. JADE: a FIPA2000 compliant agent development environment. In: Proceedings of the Fifth International Conference on Autonomous Agents. ACM; 2001. pp. 216-217

[29] Eclipse Platform Technical Review, Object Technology International Inc. 2003

[30] Chakravart IM, Laha R, Roy J. Handbook of Methods of Applied Statistics, Volume I. John Wiley; 1967

Chapter 3

Multi-Agent System Approach for Trustworthy Cloud Service Discovery

Akinwale Akinwunmi, Emmanuel Olajubu and
Ganiyu Aderounmu

Additional information is available at the end of the chapter

http://dx.doi.org/10.5772/intechopen.84291

Abstract

Accessing the advantages of cloud computing requires that a prospective user has proper access to trustworthy cloud services. It is a strenuous and laborious task to find resources and services in a heterogeneous network such as cloud environment. The cloud computing paradigm being a form of distributed system with a complex collection of computing resources from different domains with different regulatory policies but having a lot of values could enhance the mode of computing. However, a monolithic approach to cloud service discovery cannot help the necessities of cloud environment efficiently. This study put forward a distributive approach for finding sincere cloud services with the use of Multi-Agents System for ensuring intelligent cloud service discovery from trusted providers. Experiments were carried out in the study using CloudAnalyst and the results indicated that extending the frontiers MAS approach into cloud service discovery by way of integrating trust into the process improves the quality of service in respect of response time and scalability. A further comparative analysis of the Multi-Agents System approach for cloud service discovery to monolithic approach showed that Multi-Agents System approach is highly efficient, and highly flexible for trustworthy cloud service discovery.

Keywords: cloud services, multi-agent system, service discovery, distributed system, functional analysis

1. Introduction

Cloud Computing offers and delivers computing resources as services such as servers, storage, databases, networking, software, analytics and a lot more over the Internet. The collection of these resources is dynamically provided according to service-level agreements negotiated

among cloud service provider and consumer [1]. It offers a replacement computing model in which resources like power, storage and online applications are shared as 'services' over the net [2]. It is an archetype that depends on sharing data and computations over an ascendable network of nodes. The nucleus of the nodes revolves round end user computers, data centers, and cloud services. Such a collection of nodes is defined as a cloud [3]. Cloud is a distributed system with a fancy aggregation of computing resources from various domains with different management policies however having vast edges that would enhance the mode of computing [4].

Cloud Computing is among the next generation in computing [5]. It is closely related to previous, well-known distributed computing initiatives such as Web services and grid computing [6]. It relies on sharing computing resources in which having local servers or personal devices to handle applications are not required.

Clouds point to computational resources that are accessible as scalable, on demand, pay as-you-go services provided in the Internet. It makes accessible infrastructure, platform, and software as subscription-based services in a pay-as-you-go manner to users. The basic classifications for the services are namely; Infrastructure as a Service (IaaS), Platform as a Service (PaaS), and Software as a Service (SaaS) in industries [7]. However, a number of other classifications have been derived from these basic classifications.

Some examples of the cloud services are email services in which users gain access to their email hosted "in the cloud" from any computing device with a browser and enabled Internet connection. This is a departure from the traditional local hosting of email services. With innovations in cloud computing today, a number of Web apps like VoIP for making free voice call on the Internet, social networking solutions for social connection online, online media services for multimedia content viewing and sharing, financial apps and many more applications are deployed on the cloud. Even traditional desktop software, such as Microsoft Office suite has been deployed on the cloud as a service.

As stated in [8], cloud computing has the potential to add value to organizations, industries, and global economy by:

- Spontaneously accelerating the way companies innovate on products and services, supporting team product development by collaborating professionals globally with access to more powerful and economical computing resources
- Speeding up the ability of organizations to mine their data for data analytics
- Giving access to information technology for all sizes and shapes of organizations
- Assisting in advancing a virile and highly competitive global economy

In a multi-facets atmosphere like cloud that hosts thousands of service instances, discovering cloud services is an infinite task owning to the very fact that there are massive types of services from varied providers having completely different levels of quality of service.

A service discovery system which will ensure the correctness and completeness of discovery is related to having trustworthy cloud services in cloud atmosphere than in an exceedingly tiny restricted and same atmosphere. Completeness of service discovery depends on the ability of the system to intelligently show relevant results from across the outlined boundaries and across potentially-wide network distances. Likewise a high level of correctness is needed in order that the relevant results do not stray amidst a flood of a probably vast range of irrelevant results [9]. A monolithic approach to service discovery cannot support the distinctiveness of the cloud surroundings that is distributed across the varied domain boundaries and across completely different heterogeneous networks. Therefore, a distributive approach to cloud service discovery that is trustworthy is highly desired. Multi-Agents System (MAS) approach for cloud service discovery will assist greatly in addressing the challenge of discovering a trustworthy cloud service. MAS is an aggregation of multiple autonomous (intelligent) agents which collectively cooperate together for solving a distributed task such as cloud service discovery.

2. Service discovery system

Resource discovery is any mechanism that is providing capabilities to locate a service. Service discovery is a part of resource discovery and it is envisioned as the competence to find certain services such as applications or clearly outlined network services which are not pure conjectures [10].

Finding resources in an exceedingly giant scale, multi-domain network could be a non-trivial task [4]. There is also several providers, each with totally different characteristics, therefore providing a spread of varied levels of user-requirement suitableness [9]. In order to create awareness regarding the standing and also the handiness of those resources, a Service Discovery (SD) mechanism should be put in place. All the service providers are needed to register in such a mechanism, together with all the mandatory information like the service uniform resource locator (URL), rates, compatibility and service interface in order to expose the services to the would be users [9]. A matchmaking of the client requested service with available resources is done by the information service and the results is returned to the requester. **Figure 1** shows a top-level overview of SD's generic architecture.

A Service Discovery System provides a mechanism for:

i. services to register their availability

ii. locating a single instance of a particular service

iii. notifying when the instances of a service change

User requirement are used as input for discovering the best suited cloud services among various repositories of cloud providers [11].

Service and resource discovery are crucial to support any service infrastructure like cloud computing. A large-scale, multi-domain service infrastructure requires a service discovery system that is open, scalable, robust and efficient to a greater extent than a single-domain system [12].

In a heterogeneous environment such as cloud in which thousands of service instances are hosted, the correctness and completeness of discovery are very important than in a small, homogeneous environment [12].

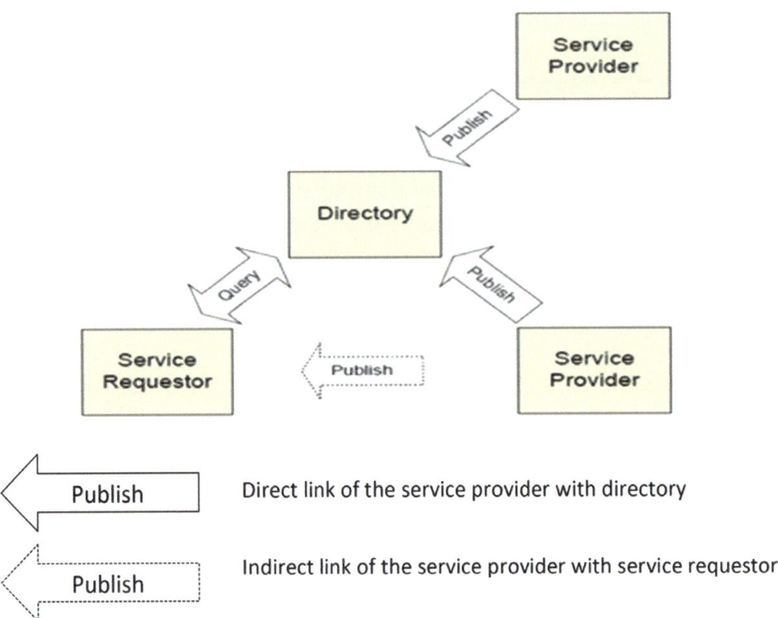

Figure 1. Service discovery generic architecture (source: [9]).

In most suitable circumstances, the exactness measures of a service discovery system would make sure that the results response clearly agrees with the intent of the user query, even with the multifariousness that may exist in the information representation and syntax of each service discovery domain. The search mechanism used determines the level of completeness and the service description expressiveness and query languages used determines the correctness [12].

Service discovery in cloud environment is made challenging by the potentially large number of available heterogeneous services and service providers. Service discovery is further complicated by the varied level of quality of service (QoS) offered by the providers. Security concern is also a big challenge while looking for an appropriate cloud service.

3. Trust

TRUST simply means act of faith that relies on confidence that something will surely be delivered as promised [13, 14]. A system is trusted less if it gives insufficient information about its expertise. Mere claims such as "secure cloud" or "trust me" do not help much to boost the trust level of consumers unless enough information is presented with the services. Establishing a trusted relationship between the service provider and the customer is one of the main issues cloud computing faces today. The potential customers are not sure whether the management of the service is trustworthy or if there is any risk of insider attacks within the service provider enclave.

Trust has been described in various fields such as psychology, sociology, and economics. Many authors have given different meanings to trust and categorized it based on these different meaning. Researchers have focused on trust over a long time [15], trust between humans has been examined to the effects of trust in economic transactions among the social scientists [16–18]. The concept of trust can be easily understood, but it has not been seemly defined.

Control is an important factor in trust. If control over the assets, a system has cannot be ascertain then such is system cannot be trusted. Preventing a trust violation in cloud computing should be the concern and not guaranteeing compensation when it does happen. No compensation can guarantee the restoration of the lost data or the organization's reputation, a security breach of data is irredeemable. A trust model for cloud computing must thus focus substantially on preventing breach occurrence than on post-breach compensation [19].

New technology must steadily acquire its reputation for good performance and security, winning users' trust over time [19]. Trust is derived from the reputation of an entity. Based on the reputation derived, a level of trust is imparted upon an entity [20]. Hence, trust in a cloud service provider results to perceived usefulness or other positive perceptions of the cloud service provider's activities. Trust will positively have effect on the desire to use cloud services and the quality of prior experience will positively influence building trust in cloud service provider's ability. The scope of previous experience will determine the relationship between trust and intention to use cloud technology. Trust is an established factor needed for attaining success in open and dynamic cloud environment for intelligent cloud service delivery.

4. Agent-based service discovery

A multi-agent system is a distributed system having multiple software agents, which create "a loosely coupled network, called a multi-agent system (MAS), to work together to solve problems that they are not capable of handling as an entity" [21]. Multi-agent systems are a community of autonomous agents working together in order to achieve a task [22]. In MAS the individual agent shows critical insight and self-rule. There have been application of MAS technologies in addressing challenges in a number of distributed systems like scientific computing and information fusion over the years [23–25].

Despite the fact that there are various contrasts between cloud computing and multi-agent systems, both are two distributed computing frameworks, in this manner a few common issues can be distinguished and a lot more qualities can be determined by the joined utilization of cloud computing and multi-agents systems [26]. There have been a number of attempts in using agent technology in solving problems that exist in cloud computing.

Kang and Sim [27] in their research exhibited a four-stage, agent-based cloud service discovery protocol. In the protocol, negotiation agents, brokering agents and information agents were used for reinforcing the resource management system due to their scalability and adaptability attributes. In order to automate and coordinate resource management to activities self-organizing agents were used. Furthermore, the disparity in kind of the resources is basic in heterogeneous frameworks like the cloud. In the research, although MAS approach was used but the issue of trust was not considered among the cloud entities while cloud services were been discovered [27]. Also matching of the request with available service was only focused in the brokering process and not in the final service deployed for use.

Han and Sim [28] introduced a Cloud Service Discovery System (CSDS) that upheld the cloud users in finding a cloud service over the Internet. The CSDS) prototype has a search engine with three different agents namely; Query Processing Agent, Filtering Agent, and Cloud Service Reasoning Agent (CSRA). It has two components namely a CSDS which helps to discover the best cloud service on behalf of users and a cloud ontology which consists of taxonomy of definitions of different cloud services to confer with the CSRA. Added to these components was a user interface through which the user enters queries containing a service name and requirements considered by their predisposition. The CSDS with the cloud ontology outperformed the CSDS without the cloud ontology from the empirical findings. The critical reasoning made possible by cloud ontology component enabled the CSDS to be more successful in finding cloud services that matches users' preference [28]. There were partially implementation of query processing, filtering and rating functionalities but trust was not considered as a concern in the process.

An agent-based cloud system for cloud service reservation was also worked on by Gopinadh and Saravanan [29]. The system consists of an agent-based cloud service discovery approach that consults ontology to retrieve information about cloud services and carried out Price and Timeslot Negotiation (PTN) for cloud service reserved. The target was for getting cloud service that has best price and timeslot. The study contributed majorly an agent-based search engine for cloud service discovery using agent-based Price and Timeslot Negotiation mechanisms adapted for cloud service negotiation. The reasoning about the relations of cloud services, rating the search results and designing and construction of cloud ontology was enabled by the Cloud Service Reasoning Agent (CSRA). Multiple proposals in a negotiation round that generate aggregated utility, differing only in terms of individual price and time-slot utilities were made by the cloud agents [29]. Matters relating to trustworthiness of cloud services was not a focus in the study.

A testbed was presented by Sim [30] which is agent-based, the test-best supports the cloud resources discovery and Service Level Agreement (SLA) negotiation. The cloud resource management testbed has the following identified components for setting up the simulation instances (a) a collection of resource consumers, (b) a collection of physical machines, (c) a collection of cloud resources (virtualized machines), and (d) a collection of middleware comprising of provider agents and consumer agents *standing* as intermediaries between resource providers and consumers, respectively, and a collection of broker agents that links resource requests from consumers to advertisements from providers. The idea of e-commerce connection algorithm used for connecting buyers and sellers was used for transforming the cloud resource discovery process into a process of matching consumers' resource requests to resources of providers. The process entails a four-tier of selection, evaluation, filtering, and recommendation, such that a collection of broker agents matches consumers' requests to advertisements from providers. After effective matching of requests to resources, consumer and provider agents then agree for mutually acceptable resource time slots through negotiation [30]. It is observed that the study was making effort to lay foundation for cloud resource management that are agent-based. Trust issues between the consumers and providers were not considered on the testbed.

Ontology relationships were used by Talia [26] for the development of a multi agent based system in finding the equivalence between queries from the user and resources available from different service providers. The system utilizes agent approach due to their being autonomous and highly mobile for effective communication in a distributed environment. Therefore,

Requestor Agent, Mapper Agent, and Search Agent - and a search engine constitute the system. Java Agent Development Framework was used for agents' development. A concept based search using similarity reasoning from the ontology relationships of the concepts in the cloud ontology was adopted by the search engine. The average waiting time for a search was optimized as a result of multiple agents employed [26]. The possibility of finding a perfect match was enhanced due to the use of ontology.

Cloud ontology technique was utilized by Rajendran and Swamynathan [31] for efficient discovery of cloud services. In the technique, multi-broker agent that consults ontology was used in the discovery of cloud services in the process of retrieving information about services. The technique resulted to having a Cloud Service Discovery using Broker Agents (CSDBA). The approach combines the merits of the agent-based system and the semantic matching mechanism using cloud ontology notably in reasoning about the relations of cloud services. It was designed to enable consumers find the required cloud services. CSDBA was highly successful than traditional approach in finding cloud services that matches users' requirement. In the future, there is likelihood of extending cloud services brokering method as well as improved method the supports cloud crawling and rate the services based on QoS [31].

Based on the literatures reviewed, attempting to use MAS in cloud service discovery has been ongoing but adequate attention was not given to issues on trustworthiness of cloud service in the process tackling the issue will greatly improve the process. This work is depending on the capabilities of the MAS to extend the discovery system to ensure that trustworthy cloud services are discovered for use by the potential users. Adding the multi-agent paradigm for trustworthy cloud service discovery will enable efficient cloud service discovery and enhance the process.

5. System design

Functional Analysis was used in the conceptual design for a trustworthy cloud service discovery system. Functional Analysis is a crucial tool for the design of process to explore new concepts and to define their architectures in system engineering [32]. The functional requirements for a trustworthy cloud service discovery system was define using this tool. It made sure that all necessary components were added and unrequired components were exempted. The interdependency among the system components were also determined and stated. The major steps of Functional Analysis were made up of the functional tree, the functions/devices matrix and the product tree. Starting from the functional tree and in particular by way of identifying the basic functions, the system's functional requirements were defined, and the building blocks of the system were determined using the product tree, thus this give rise to the system's functional architecture. Following the Functional Analysis approach, the building block for trustworthy cloud service discovery using multi-agent approach was identified. This led to the new proposed cloud service discovery system, and their integration to build up its functional framework. Therefore the following fundamental subsystems are required to achieve efficient cloud service discovery namely: Cloud User subsystem, Cloud Provider subsystem, Trust Evaluator subsystem, Broker subsystem and Database as depicted in **Figure 2**. The various identified subsystems must work together effectively for realizing a cloud service discovery system that is trustworthy.

5.1. System architecture

The distributed system architecture for cloud service discovery was formed from the integration of the different basic components of the functional block [33]. The architecture is three tiered as shown in **Figure 3**.

i. Application and resource layer

ii. Agent layer

iii. Database layer

5.1.1. Application and resource layer

The layer is the aggregation of all cloud services available and it provides the interface for connecting to the various cloud resources and services. The cloud services are categorized based on the basic cloud service models. A cloud service is any resource that is made available via the Internet. The most prevalent cloud service resources are Software as a Service (SaaS), Platform as a Service (PaaS) and Infrastructure as a Service (IaaS). SaaS is a form of software accessible model where applications are hosted by a vendor or service provider and made available to customers over a network, typically the Internet. PaaS has to do with the delivery of operating systems and associated services over the Internet without downloads or installation. IaaS entails outsourcing the equipment used to support operations, including storage, hardware, servers and networking components, all of which are made accessible over a network.

5.1.2. Agent layer

The system was constructed based on the multi-agent approach for ensuring effective and reliable discovery. The agents are responsible for achieving intelligence in the system, such that it is more adaptive, flexible, and autonomic in its operation.

In this layer the various agents that are involved in trustworthy cloud service discovery are situated. The agents are: cloud user agents (CUA), trust evaluator agents (TEA), cloud provider agents (CPA) and cloud broker agents (CBA).

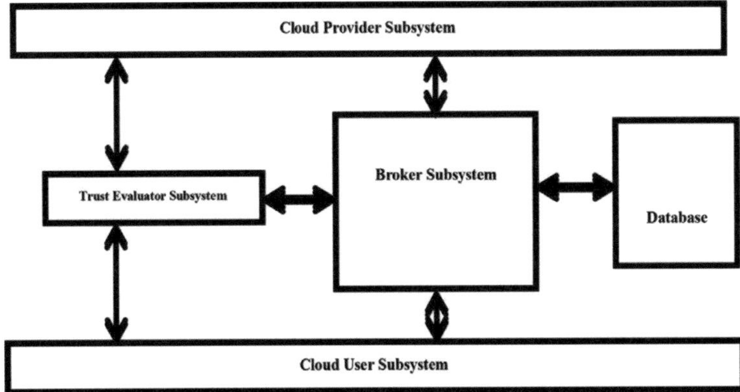

Figure 2. Functional block diagram for cloud service discovery [32].

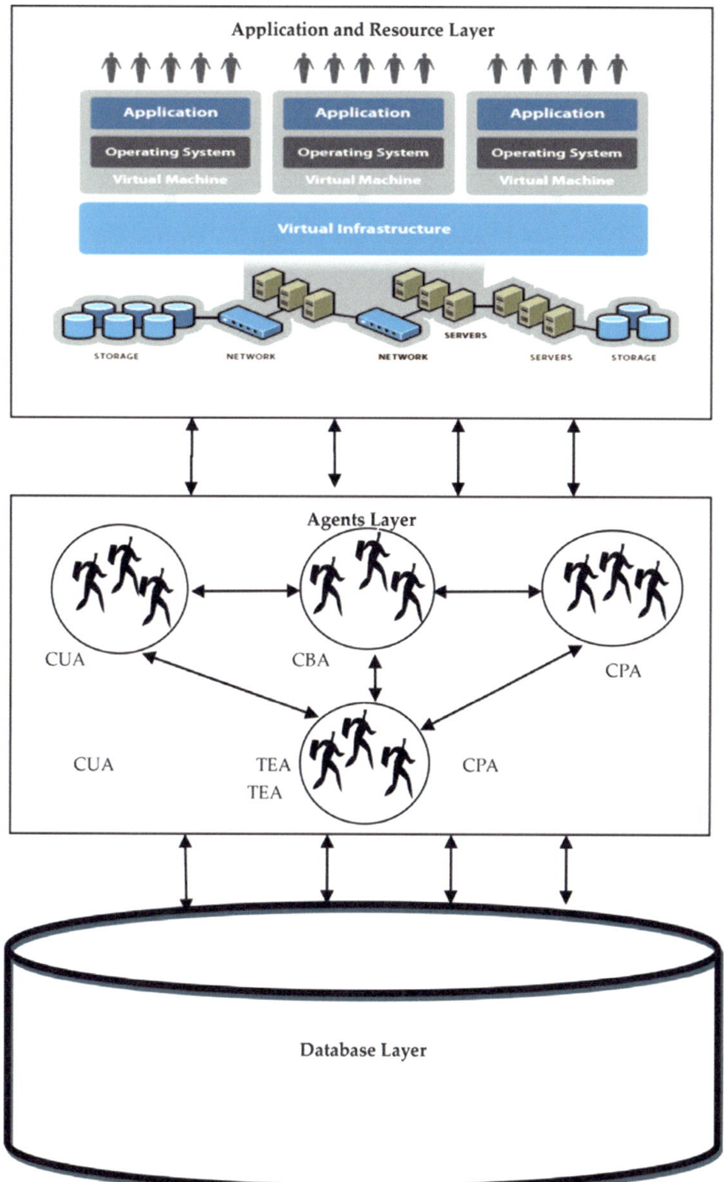

Figure 3. System architecture [32].

These autonomous agents with their specified functions establish appropriate link among one another for efficient cloud service discovery. In achieving this, a peer-to-peer approach is used among the different agents for the discovery. The cooperating agents, referred to as a peer, functions as a client with a layer of server functionality in their operations. This allows the peer to act both as a client as well as a server within the context of a given cloud service discovery scenario. Interaction may spread among all the peers, and peers can communicate directly with each other, and hence, they are constantly aware of each other, or they may communicate indirectly through other peers for effective discovery.

5.1.2.1. Agents functions

The functions of the various agents required for ensuring a trustworthy cloud service discovery are as follows [33]:

5.1.2.1.1. User agent

The user agent accepts the user's service request and the send the request to broker agents using message passing and displays the results to user through a user interface. User agent interacts with provider agent through the broker agents for service usage. Likewise the user agent interacts with the trust evaluator agent to keep track of the performance value of the provider in terms of service type, service integrity and service accessibility in a bid to build trust.

5.1.2.1.1.1. Algorithm for User agent

1. Begin

2. Let H=total number of users request within a specified time

3. Do

4. For j=1,j++,H

5. User_Agent ←User's request: UR_j

6. Broker_Agent for UR_j discovery ←User_Agent

7. Wait for Broker_Agent

8. User_Agent ←Broker_Agent returns Result of UR_j discovery

9. User Interface ←User_Agent Result for use

10. If (UR_j is used) Then

11. User_Agent interacts with Trust_Evaluator_Agent on UR_j

12. End if

13. Next j

14. While(User's request≠⊘)

15. Stop

5.1.2.1.2. Broker agent

The analysis of the user's request in order to determine its type is done by the broker agent. It attempts to find a close match for the identified service request and sends the list of such services to the user agent. It forwards user-provider's interaction information to the database. It also confers with database for other broker agent recommendation. The broker agent gets trust value updates from trust evaluator agent.

5.1.2.1.2.1. User agent and Broker agent interaction algorithm

1. Begin
2. If (*Broker_Agent received User_Agent Message*) Then
3. Broker_Agent Analyse UR_j
4. Search the database for a match
5. If (*UR_j match is found*) then
6. Broker_Agent ←UR_{jmatch}
7. Else
8. Other_Broker_Agents ←UR_i
9. If (*UR_j match is found by Other_Broker_Agents*) Then
10. Broker_Agent ←UR_{jmatch}
11. Else
12. Broker_Agent ←UR_{jmiss}
13. End if
14. End if
15. User_Agent ←Broker_Agent
16. End if
17. Stop

5.1.2.1.2.2. Broker agent and Trust evaluator agent interaction algorithm

1. Begin
2. Do
3. Broker_Agent Interact with Trust_Evaluator_ Agent
4. Broker_Agent ← Trust_Evaluator_ Agent (trust value updates)
5. Database ←Broker_Agent(Stores user agent – provider agent interaction information)
6. While (*a typical service is in use*)
7. Stop

5.1.2.1.3. Trust evaluator agent

It follows and keeps track of the provider service provider's behaviour contributing to a proper operation of the cloud in terms of the following factors: service type, service integrity, and service availability and accessibility by interacting with user and provider agents. It determines the trustworthiness of cloud service provider. It has a table for holding the performance of the provider and updates it when new performance value is available.

5.1.2.1.3.1. Algorithm

1. Begin
2. Do
3. Trust_Evaluator_ Agent: Monitors provider's performance
4. Trust_Evaluator_ Agent: Computes the trustworthiness of providers
5. Broker_Agent ← Trust_Evaluator_ Agent (sends trust value updates)
6. Trust_Evaluator_ Agent: Stores the providers' performance
7. While (*User_Agent Interacts with Provider_Agent*)

   Stop

5.1.2.1.4. Provider agent

At each cloud service provider site, provider agents are available. They send advertisement, removal and updates information of cloud services to the broker agent. It makes services available for use by the user agent.

5.1.2.1.4.1. Algorithm

1. Begin
2. Do
3. Provider_Agent : Create service instance
4. Broker_Agent ← Provider_Agent (Sends service availability information)
5. Broker_Agent ← Provider_Agent (Sends service expire information)
6. Broker_Agent ← Provider_Agent (Sends service update information)
7. User_Agent ← Provider_Agent (Offers service)
8. While (*a service is being offered by service provider)*
9. Stop

The agents' operations class diagram and sequence diagram are depicted in **Figure 4** and **5** respectively.

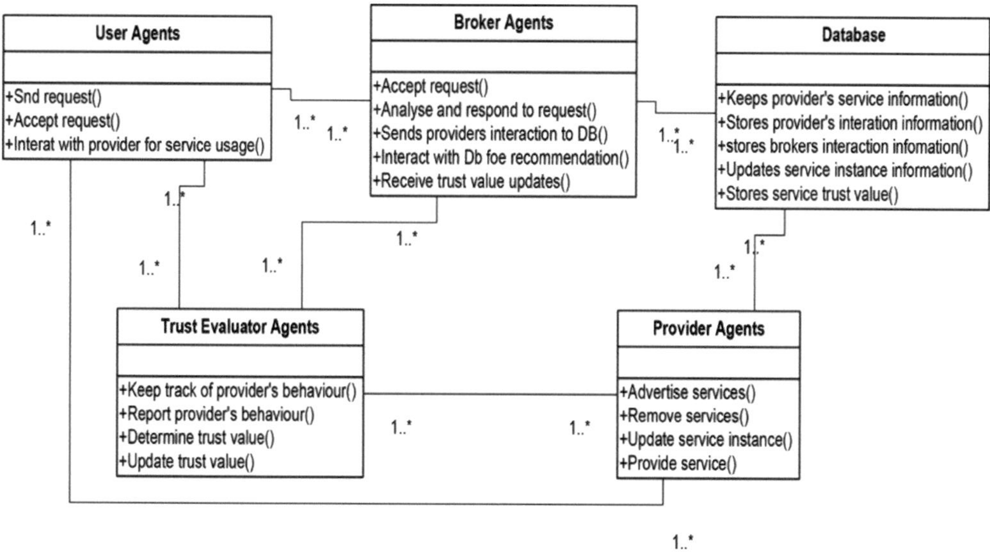

Figure 4. Agents' operations class diagram.

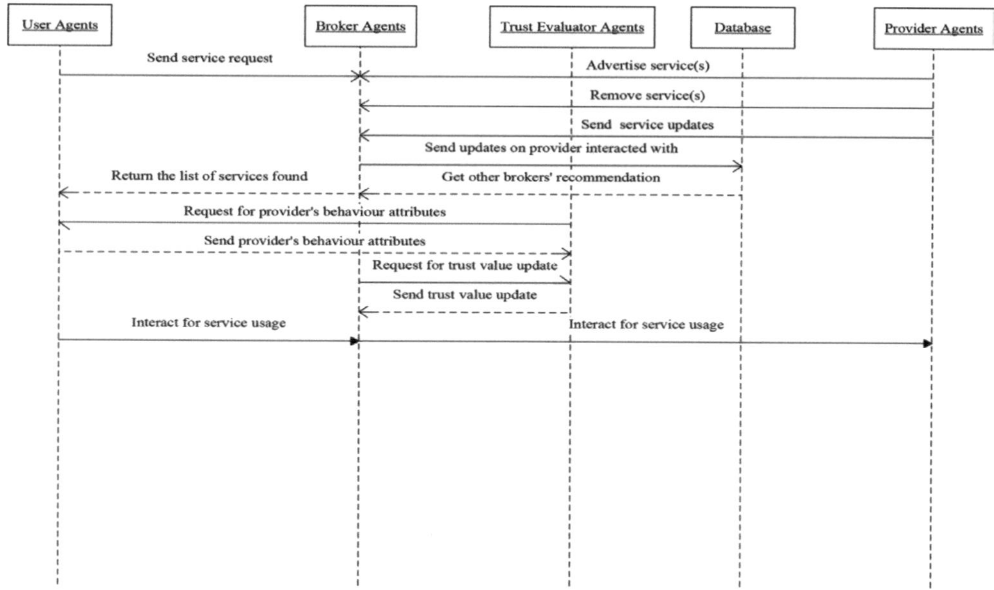

Figure 5. Agents' operations sequence diagram.

5.2. Database layer

The database layer holds the details of service usage and agents interaction information. It contains service information and trust value rating for providers. It also maintains the broker's interaction information. In a basic cloud service discovery system, user submit their request to the broker. The broker confer with the registry or directory to find a possible match for the user's request. The provider publishes the instances of its available services inside the service registry or service directory and from time to time gives updates of the status of the published service [33].

6. Experiments setups, outcomes and discussions

Simulation experiments were carried out to unravel the impact of extending MAS approach to achieve a trustworthy cloud service discovery using response time and scalability as the performance metrics [33]. The response time is the time lag from the instant of service request by the users to the instant of having the result of the service requested. This is dependent on round trip time (RTT) and the users load (UL). Scalability is a factor that considers how the system can be easily adjusted in such a way to accept changes in the number of users, resources and computing entities attached to it. Scalability (S) is dependent on processing capability of the provider which is define in terms of the processing time (PT) and users load (UL).

The experiment considered the cloud service discovery transactions conducted without involving trust factor against the same kind of cloud service discovery transaction involving trust factor in order to investigate their difference. CloudAnalyst [34] was used to model and analyze large scale cloud computing buildup in the simulations conducted. Considering the nature of throttled load balancing policy of the CloudAnalyst, the integration of trust capability in cloud environment was achieved with this policy while the round-robin load balancing policy, was used for specifying cloud transaction without trust integration [33].

The first experiment conducted depicted cloud service discovery scenario using CloudAnalyst. In this instance, there were 5,10,15,20, 25 and 30 identified groups of users agents in addition to diversified cloud provider agents and the user agent growth factor varied from 100 to 10,000,000. These units of user agents were created randomly using Poisson distribution by changing the number of users in a realistic manner. The user agents represent the potential users attempting to find cloud service that meet their requirement while the provider agents represent the various cloud service providers with their different cloud service models. The detailed configuration for the experiment were shown in **Table 1**. In this experiment, the number of user agents' growth factor were varied while the number of the provider agent was varied in order to observe the behaviour of the previous system without trust integration and proposed system with trust integration in respect of the response time.

Table 2 depicts the results obtained from the simulation experiment. The graph shown in **Figure 6** has the plot of the round trip time against the number of user agents to ascertain the behaviour of the proposed and previous systems in respect of response time. From the results, the previous system has higher response time while the proposed system has lower and refined stable response time. The percentage difference of the systems' response time shown in **Table 2** attested to this. The experiment revealed that the proposed system has lower response time of as a result of trust integration.

The second simulation experiment was also conducted for cloud service discovery transaction using CloudAnalyst. In the simulation scenario there were 5, 10, 15, 20, 25 and 30 groups of

User agents	Provider agent	User growth factor	Request growth factor	Execution instruction per length
5	1	100	10	100
10	2	1000	10	100
15	3	10,000	10	100
20	4	100,000	10	100
25	5	1,000,000	10	100
30	6	10,000,000	10	100

Table 1. Simulation parameter configurations for varied number of user agents' growth factor and varied number of provider agents in response time test.

User agents growth factor	Round trip time (ms) (existing system)	Round trip time (ms) (proposed system)	Percentage difference (%)
100	302.12	300.81	−0.434
1000	302.42	300.19	−0.737
10,000	303.10	301.15	−0.643
100,000	303.10	301.08	−0.666
1,000,000	303.71	301.13	−0.849
10,000,000	303.49	301.40	−0.689

Table 2. Results of varied number of user agents' growth factor and varied number of provider agents for response time test.

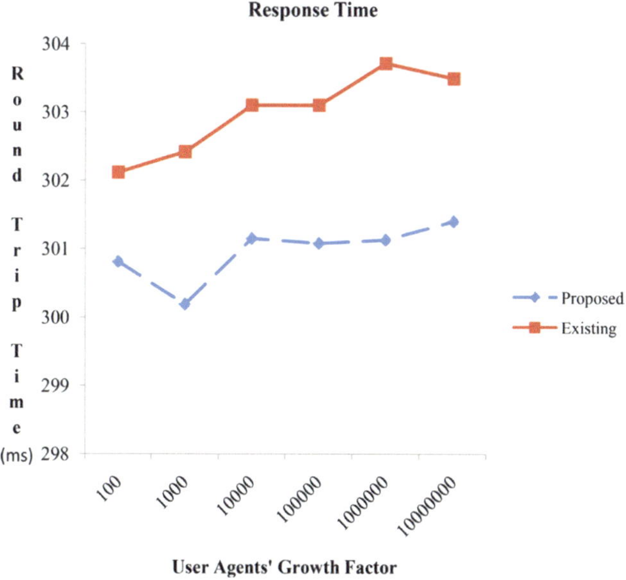

Figure 6. Varied number of user agents' growth factor and varied number of provider agents in response time experiment.

user agents with varied number cloud provider agents having a capacity of 5 virtual machines each. Similarly, the user agents represent the potential users attempting to find cloud service that meet their requirement while the provider agents represent the various cloud service providers with their different cloud service models. The user agents' growth factor was varied from 100 to 10,000,000. **Table 3** contains parameter configuration for the experiment.

In this experiment, the value for user agent growth factor was varied as well as the population of the provider agent with a view to determine the behaviour of the previous system without trust integration and proposed system with trust integration for scalability test.

Table 4 shows the outcomes from the experiment conducted. The graph in **Figure 7** depicts the plot of the provider agent processing time against the number of user agents' growth factor to verify the behaviour of the proposed and previous systems in terms of scalability. From the outcomes, the trust integration in the proposed system aid it to scale the request of user agents reasonably better than the previous system as the population of user agents moves up and the processing capability of each of the provider agents stays firm. The percentage difference of the systems' scalability metric as shown in **Table 4** evidently attested to this.

User agents	Provider agents	Number of virtual machines	User growth factor	Request growth factor	Execution instruction per length
5	1	5	100	10	100
10	2	5	1000	10	100
15	3	5	10,000	10	100
20	4	5	100,000	10	100
25	5	5	1,000,000	10	100
30	6	5	10,000,000	10	100

Table 3. Simulation parameter configuration for varied number of user agents' growth factor and varied number of provider agents in scalability test.

User agents growth factor	Provider agent processing time (ms) (existing system)	Provider agent processing time (ms) (proposed system)	Percentage difference (%)
100	1.91	0.59	−69.110
1000	2.60	0.38	−85.385
10,000	2.87	0.92	−67.944
100,000	2.98	0.95	−68.121
1,000,000	2.95	0.37	−87.458
10,000,000	3.06	0.97	−68.301

Table 4. Varied number of user agents' growth factor and varied number of provider agents for scalability.

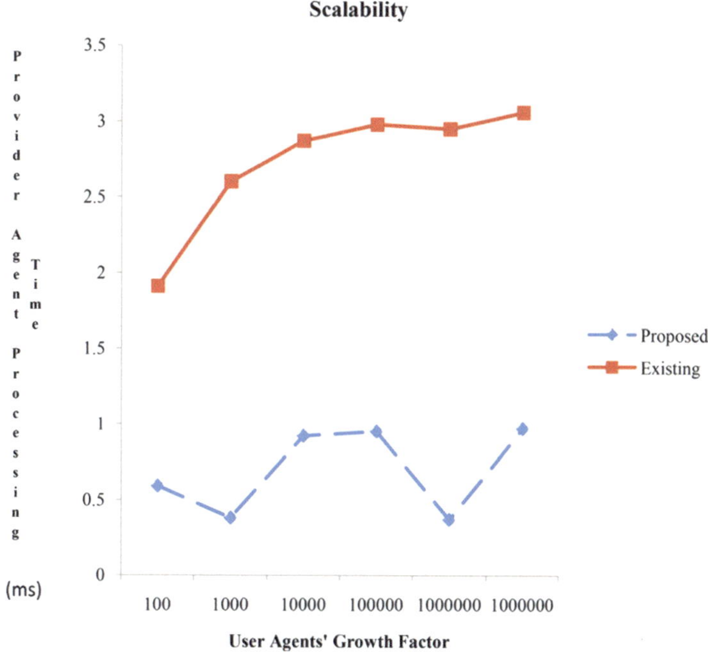

Figure 7. Varied number of user agents' growth factor and varied number of provider agents for scalability.

6.1. Validation of simulation experiment results

From the experiments, the proposed system having trust integration outperformed the previous one without trust. The results validation was achieved by applying paired difference t –test to the percentage difference of the response time for the proposed and the previous systems with each having six group sizes in the simulation configuration. The Null hypothesis opines that there is no significant difference between the proposed and previous system but the alternative hypothesis states that there is significant difference between them.

The calculated t values for the response time in the simulation done resulted to −70.43. The total group size of six (6) has a degree of freedom of five (5). A table t value of 2.02 (one-tailed, a significance level (α) of 0.05) using 5 degrees of freedom (df), at 95% confidence interval was obtained. Comparing the absolute calculated t value to the tabled t showed that the proposed system which has lower response time is significantly different ($p = 0.05$) from the previous system owning to trust integration in it.

Carrying out a similar t –test on the percentage difference of the scalability metric with six group size in the simulation settings for the proposed and the previous systems, resulted to the calculated t values of −3.09. Using a t table with 5 degrees of freedom (df) and confidence level of 95%, the table t value is 2.02 (one-tailed, a significance level (α) of 0.05). It is observed that absolute calculated t value of 3.09 was more than the table t value revealing that the proposed system is more scalable and significantly different ($p = 0.05$) from the previous system due to trust integration in it.

7. Comparative analysis

The MAS implementation for cloud service discovery supports the interconnection and interoperation of the autonomous interacting agents in the cloud environment. The MAS provides for efficient retrieving and filtering of trustworthy cloud services based on user's preference. **Table 5** gives a summary of the comparative analysis of the monolithic approach to cloud service discovery and the distributive approach using MAS.

S/n	Comparison factor	Monolithic	Distributive
1.	Computational efficiency	Less efficient	Highly efficient
2.	Reliability	Less reliable	Highly reliable
3.	Extensibility	Difficult to extend	Easy to extend
4.	Robustness	Less robust	Highly robust
5.	Maintainability	Difficult to maintain	Easy to robust
6.	Responsiveness	Slow response	Quick response
7.	Flexibility	Less flexible	Highly flexible
8.	Reusability	Difficult to reuse	Easy to reuse

Table 5. Comparative analysis of the monolithic approach to cloud service discovery and the distributive approach using MAS.

8. Conclusion

The cloud computing is a form of distributed system paradigm with a complex aggregation of computing resources from different domains with different administrative policies but having immense benefits that could enhance the mode of computing. Accessing the benefits of cloud computing, demands that a potential user has adequate access to trustworthy cloud services. Locating resources and services in a heterogeneous network such as cloud environment may be a tedious and laborious task. Trust is a predicated factor for achieving success in open and dynamic cloud environment for intelligent cloud service delivery. A distributive approach using MAS for trustworthy cloud service discovery was proposed in this study. The experiments were carried out and the results indicated that extending the MAS approach into cloud service discovery by way of integrating trust into the process improves the quality of service in respect of response time and scalability. The research showed that using multi-agent systems in the cloud environment aids intelligent cloud service discovery despite the nature of the cloud environment. Comparing MAS approach for cloud service discovery against the monolithic approach of cloud service discovery revealed that the approach is efficient and ensures flexibility for trustworthy cloud service discovery. It has capability to provide reliable result in a heterogeneous space where resources are spread whereas a monolithic approach is not efficient and reliable for a distributed environment such as cloud. The result of this work can be integrated into the interface between cloud consumer and cloud provider while finding trustworthy cloud services.

Author details

Akinwale Akinwunmi[1]*, Emmanuel Olajubu[2] and Ganiyu Aderounmu[2]

*Address all correspondence to: akinwale.akinwunmi@bowenuniversity.edu.ng

1 Computer Science and Information Technology Department, Bowen University, Iwo, Nigeria

2 Computer Science and Engineering Department, Obafemi Awolowo University, Ile-Ife, Nigeria

References

[1] Buyya R, Yeo CS, Venugopal S. Market-oriented cloud computing: Vision, hype, and reality for delivering IT services as computing utilities. In: Proceedings of the 10th IEEE International Conference on High Performance Computing and Communications (HPCC 2008). Dalian, China; 2008. DOI: 10.1109/HPCC.2008.172

[2] Vaquero LM, Rodero-Merino L, Caceres J, Lindner M. A break in the clouds: Towards a cloud definition. ACM SIGCOMM Computer Communication Review. 2009;**39**(1):50-55. DOI: 10.1145/1496091.1496100

[3] Mei L, Chan WK, Tse TH. A tale of clouds: Paradigm comparisons and some thoughts on research issues. In: Proceedings of the 2008 IEEE Asia-Pacific Services Computing Conference (APSCC 2008), 2008, IEEE Computer Society Press, Los Alamitos, CA. DOI: 10.1109/APSCC.2008.168

[4] AO A, EA O, GA A. A trustworthy model for reliable cloud service discovery. International Journal of Computer Applications. 2014;**87**(16):23-30. DOI: 10.5120/15293-3962

[5] Mirzaei N. 2008. Cloud Computing, Indiana University. Available from: http://grids.ucs.indiana.edu/ptliupages/publications/ReportNarimanMirzaeiJan09.pdf [Accessed on: September 20, 2012]

[6] Cortázar GO, Zapater JJS, Sánchez FG. Adding semantics to cloud computing to enhance service discovery and access. In: Proceedings of 2012 6th Euro American Conference of Telematics and Information Systems (EATIS); 23-25 May 2012. Valencia, Spain: IEEE; 2012. pp. 1-6. DOI: 10.1145/2261605.2261639

[7] Calheiros RN, Ranjan R, Beloglazov A, De Rose CAF, Buyya R. CloudSim: A toolkit for Modeling and simulation of cloud computing environments and evaluation of resource provisioning algorithms. Software: Practice and Experience. 2011;**41**:23-50. DOI: 10.1002/spe.995

[8] World Economic Forum .2010. Exploring the future of cloud computing: Riding the next wave of technology-driven transformation. Report of World Economic Forum in Partnership with Accenture; Geneva, Switzerland

[9] Kousiouris G, Kyriazis D, Varvarigou T, Oliveros E, Mandic P. Taxonomy and state of the art of service discovery mechanisms and their relation to the cloud computing stack. In: Kyriazis D, Varvarigou T, Konstanteli K, editors. Achieving Real-Time in Distributed Computing: From Grids to Clouds. Hershey, PA: Information Science Reference; 2012. pp. 75-93. DOI: 10.4018/978-1-4666-0879-5.ch805

[10] Meshkova E, Riihijarvi J, Petrova M, Mahonen P. A survey on resource discovery mechanisms, peer-to-peer and service discovery frameworks. Computer Networks. 2008;**52**(11): 2097-2128. DOI: 10.1016/j.comnet.2008.03.006

[11] Dastjerdi AV, Buyya R. An autonomous reliability-aware negotiation strategy for cloud computing environments. In: 2012 12th IEEE/ACM International Symposium on Cluster, Cloud and Grid Computing (Ccgrid 2012) 13-16 May 2012. Ottawa, ON, Canada: IEEE; 2012. DOI: 10.1109/CCGrid.2012.101

[12] Ahmed R, Limam N, Xiao J, Iraqi Y, Boutaba R. Resource and service discovery in large-scale multi-domain networks. IEEE Communications Surveys & Tutorials. 2007;**9**(4): 2-30. DOI: 10.1109/COMST.2007.4444748

[13] Costa C, Bijlsma-Frankema K. Trust and control interrelations. Group & Organization Management. 2007;**32**(4):392-406. DOI: 10.1177/1059601106293871

[14] Lund M, Solhaug B. Evolution in relation to risk and trust management. Computer. 2010;**43**(5):49-55. DOI: 10.1109/MC.2010.134

[15] McKnight DH, Chervany NL. The Meanings of Trust. MIS research Center, Carlson School of Management, University of Minnesota. Working Paper Series (WP 96-01); 1996

[16] Ba S, Paylou PA. Evidence of the effect of trust building Technology in Electronic Markets: Price premiums and buyer behaviour. MIS Quarterly. 2002;**26**:243-268. DOI: 10.2307/4132332

[17] Dasgupta P. Trust as a commodity. In: Gambetta D, editor. Trust: Making and Breaking Cooperative Relations. Blackwell; 1988. pp. 49-72

[18] McKnight DH, Cummings LL, Chervany NL. Trust formation in new Organaizational relationships. In: October 1995 Information & Decision Sciences Workshop; Curtis L. Carlson School of Management, University of Minnesota; 1995

[19] Khan KM, Malluhi Q. Establishing Trust in Cloud Computing. IT Professional. 2010;**12**(5): 20-27. DOI: 10.1109/MITP.2010.128

[20] Momani M, Abour K, Challa S. RBATMWSN: Recursive bayesian approach to trust management in wireless sensor networks. In: In 2007 3rd International Conference on Intelligent Sensors, Sensor Networks and Information Processing(ISSNIP 2007); 3-6 December 2007. Melbourne, Australia: IEEE; 2008. pp. 347-352. DOI: 10.1109/ISSNIP.2007.4496868

[21] Durfee EH, Montogomery TA. MICE: A flexible testbed for intelligent coordination experiments. In: Proceedings of the 1989 Distributed Artificial Intelligence Workshop. 1989. pp. 25-40. DOI: 10.1.1.16.8714

[22] Wooldridge M. An Introduction to MultiAgent Systems. 2nd ed. Chichester: John Wiley and Sons; 2009

[23] Drashansky T, Houstis EN, Ramakrishnan N, Rice JR. Networked agents for scientific computing. Communications of the ACM. 1999;**42**(3):48-53. DOI: 10.1145/295685.295699

[24] Khosla R, Dillon T. Intelligent hybrid multi-agent architecture for engineering complex systems. In: 1997 Proceedings of the IEEE International Conference on Neural Networks (ICNN'97); 12-12 June 1997. Houston, Texas: IEEE; 1997. pp. 2449-2454. DOI: 10.1109/ICNN.1997.614540

[25] Honavar V, Miller L, Wong J. Distributed knowledge networks. In: Proceedings of 1998 IEEE Information Technology Conference, Information Environment for the Future (Cat. No.98EX228); 3-3 Sept. 1998. Syracuse, NY, USA: USA IEEE; 1998. pp. 87-90. DOI: 10.1109/IT.1998.713388

[26] Talia D. Cloud computing and software agents: Towards cloud intelligent services. In: Fortino G, Garro A, Palopoli L, Russo W, Spezzano G, editors. Proceedings of the 12th Workshop on Objects and Agents (WOA-2011). Italy: Rende (CS); July 4-6, 2011

[27] Kang J, Towards Agents SKM. Ontology for cloud service discovery. In: 2011 International Conference on Cyber-Enabled Distributed Computing and Knowledge Discovery; 10-12 October 2011. Beijing, China: IEEE; 2011. pp. 483-490. DOI: 10.1109/CyberC.2011.84

[28] Han T, Sim KM. An ontology–Enhanced cloud service discovery system. In: Proceedings of International Multiconference of Engineers and Computer Scientists (IMECS, 2010); 17-19 March 2010. Hong Kong: IMECS; 2010. pp. 644-649

[29] Gopinadh R, Saravanan K. Cloud service reservation using PTN mechanism in ontology enhanced agent-based system. International Journal of Engineering Trends and Technology. 2013;**4**(4):791-798. ISSN:2231-5381

[30] Sim KM. Agent-based cloud commerce. In: Proceedings of 2009 IEEE International Conference on Industrial Engineering and Engineering Management; 8-11 December. Hong Kong, China: IEEE; 2009. pp. 717-721. DOI: 10.1109/IEEM.2009.5373228

[31] Rajendran V, Swamynathan SA. Novel approach for semantic service discovery in cloud using broker agents. In: Proceedings of International Conference on Advances in Computing, Communication and Information Science (ACCIS-14); June 2014. Kollam, Kerala, India: Elsevier Publications; 2014. pp. 242-250. DOI: 10.13140/2.1.4022.6085

[32] Viola N, Corpino S, Fioriti M, Stesina F. Functional analysis in systems engineering: Methodology and applications. In: Cogan B, editor. Systems Engineering–Practice and Theory. Rijeka, Croatia: InTechOpen; 2012. pp. 3-29. DOI: 10.5772/34556

[33] Akinwunmi A, Olajub EA, Aderounmu GA. A multi-agent system approach for trustworthy cloud service discovery. Cogent Engineering. 2016;**3**(1):1-17. DOI: org/10.1080/23311916.2016.1256084

[34] Wickremasinghe B, Calheiros RN, Buyya R. CloudAnalyst: A cloudsim-based visual modeller for analysing cloud computing environments and applications. In: 2010 24th IEEE International Conference on Advanced Information Networking and Applications (AINA); 20-23 April 2010. Perth, WA, Australia: IEEE; 2010. pp. 446-452. DOI: 10.1109/AINA.2010.32

Chapter 4

Guaranteed Performance Consensus for Multi-Agent Systems

Zhong Wang

Additional information is available at the end of the chapter

http://dx.doi.org/10.5772/intechopen.80285

Abstract

The guaranteed performance of the consensus control for multi-agent systems with Lipschitz nonlinear dynamics and directed interaction topologies is investigated, where the directed interaction topology contains a spanning tree. By a special matrix transformation, guaranteed performance consensus problems are transferred into guaranteed performance stabilization problems. Then, the criterions of guaranteed performance consensus for nonlinear multi-agent systems with directed interaction topologies are obtained, and an upper bound of the introduced performance function is given. A numerical simulation is given to demonstrate the effectiveness of the proposed results. Finally, some possible topics about the guaranteed performance consensus problem for nonlinear multi-agent systems are proposed.

Keywords: guaranteed performance consensus, multi-agent system, nonlinear dynamic

1. Introduction

In the past decades, many researchers focused on consensus problems for multi-agent systems due to their wide applications, including formation control of mobile agents [1], synchronization in wireless sensor networks [2], distributed automatic generation control for cyber-physical micro-grid system [3], and rendezvous [4] or flocking [5] of multiple vehicles. After Olfati-Saber and Murray [6] proposed a theoretical framework for the consensus problem, a lot of remarkable conclusions for linear multi-agent systems were presented in the literature, respectively (see the survey papers [7–12] and the references therein). In fact, many control systems in practical applications are nonlinear. Consensus problems for multi-agent systems with nonlinear dynamic have been investigated in existing works. It should be pointed out that

exiting works about nonlinear consensus problem focused on the consensus condition under a control protocol, but the consensus regulation performance was not considered by a performance index.

With the development of the consensus control theory, the guaranteed performance consensus for the multi-agent by the guaranteed performance control approach has received more and more attentions. In the guaranteed performance consensus problems, the consensus regulation performance was explicitly considered by the guaranteed performance function. By the constraint of the performance index, the consensus control can be seen as an optimal or suboptimal problem, and the control process is more affected by choosing appropriate control parameters. In existing literatures about the guaranteed performance consensus problem, such as [11–15], the dynamic characteristic of each agent in the multi-agent systems was linear. For the linear multi-agent systems, the state-space decomposition approach was widely used to decompose the consensus and disagreement dynamics of multi-agent system, and the disagreement dynamics is the key of guaranteed performance consensus control. Moreover, the guaranteed performance consensus with other control methods has been studied, such as sampled-data control [16], fault-tolerant control [17], event-triggered control [18], tracking control [19], and impulsive control [20].

For the consensus problems of nonlinear multi-agent systems, the intercoupling relationship between the consensus and disagreement dynamics because of the nonlinear dynamic. Then, the state-space decomposition approach is not able to deal with the nonlinear consensus problems. To the best of our knowledge, there are very few research works about the guaranteed performance consensus for nonlinear multi-agent systems. Moreover, the interaction topologies in most of the existing works were undirected, and there were few works about guaranteed performance consensus problem with directed interaction topologies.

In the current chapter, the guaranteed performance consensus for multi-agent systems with nonlinear dynamics is studied by introducing a performance function. By a special matrix transformation, the guaranteed performance consensus problems are transferred into guaranteed performance stabilization problems, and some conclusions about guaranteed performance consensus for nonlinear multi-agent systems are obtained.

2. Preliminaries and problem descriptions

In the current paper, the interaction topology among all agents of multi-agent systems can be modeled by a directed graph $G = (\mathscr{V}, \mathscr{E})$, where $\mathscr{V} = \{1, 2, \cdots, N\}$ and $\mathscr{E} \subseteq \mathscr{V} \times \mathscr{V}$ represent the agent set and the directed edge set, respectively. A directed edge in a directed graph denoted as (i, j) which means that agent i can obtain information from agent j. Definite $\mathscr{W} = [w_{ij}] \in \mathbf{R}^{N \times N}$ with $w_{ij} \geq 0$ and $w_{ii} = 0$ is the adjacency matrix, where $w_{ij} > 0$ if there is a directed edge between agent i and agent j, $w_{ij} = 0$ otherwise. If $w_{ij} > 0$, agent j is called the neighbor of agent i, and all the neighbors of agent i consist of the neighboring set of agent i. A directed path is a sequence of ordered edges of the form (i_1, i_2), (i_2, i_3), $\cdots$. The Laplacian matrix of the interaction topology G is defined as $L = [l_{ij}] \in \mathbf{R}^{N\times N}$, where $l_{ii} = \sum_{j\neq i} w_{ij}$ and $l_{ij} = -w_{ij}$. In the current paper, it is assumed that the directed graph G has a directed spanning tree. The following lemma shows basic properties of the Laplacian matrix of a directed interaction graph.

Lemma 1 [21]: Let $L = [l_{ij}] \in \mathbf{R}^{N\times N}$ be the Laplacian matrix of a directed interaction graph G, then (i) L at least has a zero eigenvalue, and $\mathbf{1}_N$ is an associated eigenvector; that is, $L\mathbf{1}_N = 0$. (ii) 0 is a simple eigenvalue of L, and all the other nonzero eigenvalues have positive real parts if and only if G has a directed spanning tree, i.e., $0 = \lambda_1 < \mathrm{Re}(\lambda_2) \leq \cdots \leq \mathrm{Re}(\lambda_N)$.

In the current chapter, consider the guaranteed performance consensus problem of a group of N nonlinear agents with the dynamics of ith agent given by

$$\dot{x}_i(t) = Ax_i(t) + Mf(x_i(t)) + Bu_i(t), \tag{1}$$

where $i = 1, 2, \cdots, N$, $A \in \mathbf{R}^{d\times d}$, $B \in \mathbf{R}^{d\times p}$, $M \in \mathbf{R}^{d\times m}$ are constant real matrices, $x_i(t)$ and $u_i(t)$ are the state and the control input of the ith agent, respectively, and the function $f(\cdot) : \mathbf{R}^n \times [0, +\infty) \to \mathbf{R}^m$ is a continuously differentiable vector-valued function representing the nonlinear dynamics of the ith agent which satisfies the following condition:

$$\| f(\xi_1(t)) - f(\xi_2(t))\| \leq \alpha \|\xi_1(t) - \xi_2(t)\|, \tag{2}$$

where $\forall \xi_1(t),\ \xi_2(t) \in \mathbf{R}^d$, $t \geq 0$ and $\alpha > 0$ is a constant scalar. In the current paper, a directed graph G is used to descript the interaction. Based on local relative state information of the neighbor agents, consider the following distributed consensus protocol:

$$u_i(t) = K \sum_{j=1}^{N} w_{ij}\left(x_j(t) - x_i(t)\right), \tag{3}$$

where w_{ij} is the weight of the edge between agents j and i. Let $x(t) = \left[x_1^{\mathrm{T}}(t), x_2^{\mathrm{T}}(t), \cdots, x_N^{\mathrm{T}}(t)\right]^{\mathrm{T}}$ and $g(x(t)) = \left[f(x_1(t))^{\mathrm{T}}, f(x_2(t))^{\mathrm{T}}, \cdots, f(x_N(t))^{\mathrm{T}}\right]^{\mathrm{T}}$, and then multi-agent system Eq. (1) with consensus protocol Eq. (3) can be rewritten in a vector form as

$$\dot{x}(t) = ((I_N \otimes A) - (L \otimes BK))x(t) + (I_N \otimes M)g(x(t)). \tag{4}$$

Definite $\varepsilon(t) = \left[\varepsilon_1^{\mathrm{T}}(t), \varepsilon_2^{\mathrm{T}}(t), \cdots, \varepsilon_{N-1}^{\mathrm{T}}(t)\right]^{\mathrm{T}}$ with $\varepsilon_i(t) = x_i(t) - x_{i+1}(t)$, then existing matrix

$$H = \begin{bmatrix} 1 & -1 & 0 & \cdots & 0 & 0 \\ 0 & 1 & -1 & \cdots & 0 & 0 \\ 0 & 0 & 1 & \cdots & 0 & 0 \\ \vdots & \vdots & \vdots & \ddots & -1 & 0 \\ 0 & 0 & 0 & \cdots & 1 & -1 \end{bmatrix} \in \mathbf{R}^{(N-1)\times N},$$

such that $\varepsilon(t) = (H \otimes I_d)x(t)$. Thus, a performance function can be defined as follows:

$$J_C = \sum_{i=1}^{N-1} \int_0^{+\infty} \varepsilon_i^{\mathrm{T}}(t) Q \varepsilon_i(t) \mathrm{d}t, \tag{5}$$

where Q is a given symmetric positive matrix with appropriate dimension. The following lemmas are introduced:

Lemma 2 [22]: For a Laplacian matrix $L \in \mathbf{R}^{N \times N}$ of the graph G and the matrix H, there exists a matrix $U \in \mathbf{R}^{N \times (N-1)}$ such that $L = UH$.

Lemma 3 [22]: If G has a directed spanning tree and U is full column rank, the real part of the eigenvalue of the matrix HU satisfies $\mathrm{Re}(\lambda(HU)) > 0$, and there exist a symmetric and positive definite matrix $W \in \mathbf{R}^{(N-1) \times (N-1)}$ and a positive scalar γ such that

$$(HU)^{\mathrm{T}} W + WHU > \gamma W,$$

where $0 < \gamma < 2\min\{\mathrm{Re}(\lambda(HU))\}$.

Lemma 4 [23]: For any given $\forall \xi_1(t), \xi_2(t) \in \mathbf{R}^d$ and matrices S of appropriate dimensions, one has

$$2\xi_1{}^{\mathrm{T}}(t) S \xi_2(t) \le \xi_1{}^{\mathrm{T}}(t) \xi_1(t) + \xi_2{}^{\mathrm{T}}(t) S^{\mathrm{T}} S \xi_2(t).$$

In the squeal, the definitions of the guaranteed performance consensus and consensualization are given, respectively.

Definition 1: Multi-agent system (Eq. (4)) is said to achieve guaranteed performance consensus with the performance function (Eq. (5)) if $\lim_{t \to +\infty}(x_j(t) - x_i(t)) = 0$, and there exists a scalar $J_C^* > 0$ such that $J_C \le J_C^*$, where J_C^* is said to be an upper bound of the performance function (Eq. (5)).

Definition 2: Multi-agent system (Eq. (1)) is said to be guaranteed performance consensualizable by the consensus protocol (Eq. (2)) with the performance function (Eq. (5)), if there exists a gain matrix K such that Eq. (4) achieves guaranteed performance consensus.

Due to the definition $\varepsilon_i(t) = x_i(t) - x_{i+1}(t)$, one has $\lim_{t \to +\infty} \varepsilon(t) = 0$ if and only if $\lim_{t \to +\infty}(x_i(t) - x_{i+1}(t)) = 0$ with $i = 1, 2, \cdots, N-1$; that is, $x_1(t) = x_2(t) = \cdots = x_N(t)$ when $t \to +\infty$. Then, it is obtained that $\varepsilon(t)$ is the disagreement vector of multi-agent system (Eq. (4)). Thus, J_C in Eq. (5) represents the guaranteed performance of the consensus control for multi-agent system (Eq. (4)).

3. Analysis of guaranteed performance consensus

By $\varepsilon(t) = (H \otimes I_d) x(t)$, multi-agent system (Eq. (4)) can be transformed into

$$\dot{\varepsilon}(t) = ((I_{N-1} \otimes A) - (HU \otimes BK)) \varepsilon(t) + (I_{N-1} \otimes M) \zeta(x(t)), \tag{6}$$

where

$$\zeta(x(t)) = (H \otimes I_d)g(x(t)) = \begin{bmatrix} f(x_1(t)) - f(x_2(t)) \\ f(x_2(t)) - f(x_3(t)) \\ \vdots \\ f(x_{N-1}(t)) - f(x_N(t)) \end{bmatrix} \quad (7)$$

and the matrix U satisfies Lemmas 2 and 3. Moreover, from Eq. (3), one has $u(t) = -(L \otimes K)x(t)$ with $u(t) = \left[u_1^{\mathrm{T}}(t), u_2^{\mathrm{T}}(t), \cdots, u_N^{\mathrm{T}}(t)\right]^{\mathrm{T}}$. By $\varepsilon(t) = (H \otimes I_d)x(t)$ and Lemma 2, one has

$$u(t) = -(U \otimes K)\varepsilon(t) \quad (8)$$

For J_{C}, the performance function (Eq. (5)) can be rewritten in a vector form as

$$J_{\mathrm{C}} = \int_0^{+\infty} \varepsilon^{\mathrm{T}}(t)(I_{N-1} \otimes Q)\varepsilon(t)\mathrm{d}t. \quad (9)$$

The following result presents a sufficient condition for nonlinear multi-agent system (Eq. (4)) to achieve guaranteed performance consensus and designs the consensus control gain matrix for the distributed consensus protocol (Eq. (3)).

Theorem 1: Assume that G has a directed spanning tree. Nonlinear multi-agent system (Eq. (4)) achieves guaranteed performance consensus if there exists a symmetric and positive definite matrix $P \in \mathbf{R}^{d \times d}$ such that $\Xi < 0$, where

$$\Xi = \begin{bmatrix} \Xi_{11} & PM & \alpha I_d & Q \\ * & -\omega_{\max}^{-1} I_d & 0 & 0 \\ * & * & -\omega_{\min} I_d & 0 \\ * & * & * & -\omega_{\min} Q \end{bmatrix}$$

with

$$\Xi_{11} = A^{\mathrm{T}}P + PA - \gamma PBB^{\mathrm{T}}P,$$

$$\omega_{\min} = \min\{\lambda_i(W), i = 1, 2, \cdots, N-1\},$$

$$\omega_{\max} = \max\{\lambda_i(W), i = 1, 2, \cdots, N-1\}.$$

In this case, for the distributed consensus protocol (Eq. (3)), the consensus control gain matrix $K = B^{\mathrm{T}}P$.

Proof: Consider the following Lyapunov functional candidate:

$$V(t) = \varepsilon^{\mathrm{T}}(t)(W \otimes P)\varepsilon(t), \quad (10)$$

where $P \in \mathbf{R}^{d \times d}$ is a symmetric and positive definite matrix and W satisfies Lemma 3. Then, the time derivation of the Lyapunov functional candidate $V(t)$ along the trajectory of Eq. (6) is

$$\dot{V}(t) = 2\varepsilon^{\mathrm{T}}(t)((I_{N-1} \otimes A) - (HU \otimes BK))^{\mathrm{T}}(W \otimes P)\varepsilon(t) + 2\zeta^{\mathrm{T}}(x(t))\big(W \otimes M^{\mathrm{T}}P\big)\varepsilon(t). \tag{11}$$

Let $K = B^{\mathrm{T}}P$, and then Eq. (11) can be transformed into

$$\begin{aligned}\dot{V}(t) = \varepsilon^{\mathrm{T}}(t)\Big(W \otimes \big(A^{\mathrm{T}}P + PA\big) - \Big((HU)^{\mathrm{T}}W + WHU\Big) \otimes PBB^{\mathrm{T}}P\Big)\varepsilon(t)\\ + 2\zeta^{\mathrm{T}}(x(t))\big(W \otimes M^{\mathrm{T}}P\big)\varepsilon(t).\end{aligned} \tag{12}$$

By Lemma 4 and Eq. (2), one can see that

$$2\zeta^{\mathrm{T}}(x(t))\big(W \otimes M^{\mathrm{T}}P\big)\varepsilon(t) \le \zeta^{\mathrm{T}}(x(t))\zeta(x(t)) + \varepsilon^{\mathrm{T}}(t)\big(W^2 \otimes PMM^{\mathrm{T}}P\big)\varepsilon(t), \tag{13}$$

By Eqs. (2) and (7), one can see that

$$\zeta^{\mathrm{T}}(x(t))\zeta(x(t)) \le \alpha^2\varepsilon^{\mathrm{T}}(t)\varepsilon(t), \tag{14}$$

From Lemma 3 and Eq. (13), $\dot{V}(t)$ satisfies

$$\dot{V}(t) \le \varepsilon^{\mathrm{T}}(t)\big(W \otimes \big(A^{\mathrm{T}}P + PA - \gamma PBB^{\mathrm{T}}P + \alpha^2\omega_{\min}^{-1}I_d + \omega_{\max}PMM^{\mathrm{T}}P\big)\big)\varepsilon(t), \tag{15}$$

where the fact that

$$\omega_{\min}I_{N-1} \le W \le \omega_{\max}I_{N-1}$$

is used. $\omega_{\min}$ and $\omega_{\max}$ are the minimum and the maximum eigenvalues of W, respectively.

Define

$$\dot{\mathfrak{J}}(t) = \dot{V}(t) + \tilde{J}_{\mathrm{C}}, \tag{16}$$

where $\tilde{J}_{\mathrm{C}} \ge 0$ and

$$\tilde{J}_{\mathrm{C}} = \varepsilon^{\mathrm{T}}(t)(I_{N-1} \otimes Q)\varepsilon(t).$$

It should be pointed out that if $\dot{\mathfrak{J}}(t) \le 0$, then $\dot{V}(t) \le 0$. Then, one can see that

$$\dot{\mathfrak{J}}(t) \le \varepsilon^{\mathrm{T}}(t)\big(W \otimes \big(A^{\mathrm{T}}P + PA - \gamma PBB^{\mathrm{T}}P + \alpha^2\omega_{\min}^{-1}I_d + \omega_{\max}PMM^{\mathrm{T}}P + \omega_{\min}^{-1}Q\big)\varepsilon(t). \tag{17}$$

By the Schur complement, if $\Xi < 0$, one has

$$\dot{\mathfrak{J}}(t) \le 0$$

and $\dot{\mathfrak{J}}(t) = 0$ if and only if $\varepsilon(t) \equiv 0$. Then, by $\tilde{J}_{\mathrm{C}} \ge 0$, if $\Xi < 0$, $\dot{V}(t) \le 0$ and $\dot{V}(t) = 0$ if and only if $\varepsilon(t) \equiv 0$. Thus, $\lim_{t \to +\infty}\varepsilon(t) = 0$ holds; that is,

$$x_1(t) = x_2(t) = \cdots = x_N(t)$$

when $t \to +\infty$. Therefore, if there exists P that satisfies $\Xi < 0$, then guaranteed performance consensus for multi-agent system (Eq. (4))with $K = B^{\mathrm{T}}P$ is achieved.

When the nonlinear multi-agent system (Eq. (4)) achieves guaranteed performance consensus, the performance of consensus control is described by the performance function (Eq. (5)). Then, an upper bound of the performance function (Eq. (5)) is able to determine.

Theorem 2: Assume that G has a directed spanning tree. If nonlinear multi-agent system (Eq. (4)) with a symmetric and positive definite matrix $P \in \mathbf{R}^{d\times d}$ achieves guaranteed performance consensus, then the performance function (Eq. (5)) has an upper bound:

$$J_{\mathrm{C}}^{*} = x^{\mathrm{T}}(0)\left(H^{\mathrm{T}}WH \otimes P\right)x(0).$$

Proof: From the proof of Theorem 1, it is obtained that

$$\tilde{J}_{\mathrm{C}} \leq -\dot{V}(t) \tag{18}$$

when nonlinear multi-agent system (Eq. (4)) achieves guaranteed performance consensus. For Eq. (18), integrating both sides along with $t \in [0, +\infty)$ gives

$$J_{\mathrm{C}} = \int_0^{+\infty} \tilde{J}_{\mathrm{C}} \mathrm{d}t \leq -\int_0^{+\infty} \dot{V}(t)\mathrm{d}t. \tag{19}$$

Since $\lim_{t\to+\infty} V(t) = 0$, one has $J_{\mathrm{C}} \leq V(0)$. Thus, $J_{\mathrm{C}}^{*} = V(0)$ is an upper bound of the quadratic performance function (Eq. (5)). From Eq. (10) and $\varepsilon(t) = (H \otimes I_d)x(t)$, the result of Theorem 2 is obtained.

In the existing works [11–20], the guaranteed performance consensus problems for linear multi-agent systems have been studied. Theorem 1 gives a sufficient condition for nonlinear multi-agent system (Eq. (4)) to achieve guaranteed performance consensus. Moreover, the directed topology is considered in the current chapter, but the topologies in [11–19] were undirected, and the directed case problem was dealt with by the sampled-data control in [20].

4. Design of guaranteed performance consensus

Theorem 3: Multi-agent system (Eq. (1)) is said to be a guaranteed performance consensualizable by consensus protocol (4) if there exists d-dimensional matrix $\tilde{P} = \tilde{P}T > 0$ such that $\tilde{\Xi} < 0$, where

$$\tilde{\Xi} = \begin{bmatrix} \tilde{\Xi}_{11} & M & \alpha\tilde{P} & \tilde{P}Q \\ * & -\omega_{\max}^{-1} I_d & 0 & 0 \\ * & * & -\omega_{\min} I_d & 0 \\ * & * & * & -\omega_{\min} Q \end{bmatrix}$$

with

$$\tilde{\Xi}_{11} = \tilde{P}A^{\mathrm{T}} + A\tilde{P} - \gamma BB^{\mathrm{T}},$$

$$\omega_{\min} = \min\{\lambda_i(W), i = 1, 2, \cdots, N-1\},$$

$$\omega_{\max} = \max\{\lambda_i(W), i = 1, 2, \cdots, N-1\}.$$

In this case, the control gain matrix satisfies $K = B^{\mathrm{T}}\tilde{P}{-}1$, and the guaranteed performance function has an upper bound:

$$J_{\mathrm{C}}^{*} = x^{\mathrm{T}}(0)\left(H^{\mathrm{T}}WH \otimes \tilde{P}{-}1\right)x(0).$$

Proof: The method of changing variables is used to determine K. Pre- and post-multiplying $\Xi < 0$ by $\Pi = \mathrm{diag}\{P^{-1}, I_d, I_d, I_d\}$ and $\Pi^{\mathrm{T}} = \mathrm{diag}\{P^{-\mathrm{T}}, I_d, I_d, I_d\}$, respectively, one has

$$\begin{bmatrix} \overline{\Xi}_{11} & M & \alpha P^{-1} I_d & P^{-1}Q \\ * & -\omega_{\max}^{-1} I_d & 0 & 0 \\ * & * & -\omega_{\min} I_d & 0 \\ * & * & * & -\omega_{\min} Q \end{bmatrix} < 0$$

with $\overline{\Xi}_{11} = P^{-1}A^{\mathrm{T}} + AP^{-\mathrm{T}} - \gamma BB^{\mathrm{T}}$. Setting $\tilde{P} = P^{-1}$, one has $\tilde{\Xi} < 0$. From Theorem 1, if $\tilde{\Xi} < 0$ are feasible, then multi-agent system (Eq. (4)) can achieve consensus. Therefore, by Definition 2 and Theorem 2, the conclusion of Theorem 3 can be obtained.

Theorem 3 presents the LMI conditions for controller design of guaranteed performance consensus. The feasibility of these LMI conditions can be checked by using the MATLAB's LMI Toolbox.

5. Simulations

A nonlinear multi-agent system composed of four agents is analyzed to demonstrate the effectiveness of the proposed approach, where all agents are labeled from 1 to 4. The dynamics of each agent is described in Eq. (1) with

$$A = \begin{bmatrix} 0 & 1 \\ -1.5 & -0.6 \end{bmatrix}, \ B = \begin{bmatrix} 0 \\ 1 \end{bmatrix},$$

$$M = \begin{bmatrix} 0.7 & 0 \\ 0 & 0.9 \end{bmatrix}, \ f(x_i(t)) = \begin{bmatrix} 0.1 \sin x_i(t) \\ 0.04 \sin x_i(t) \end{bmatrix}.$$

It can be seen that $\alpha = 0.1$ in Eq. (2). The initial states of all agents are

$$x_1(0) = \begin{bmatrix} -2.2 \\ -1.5 \end{bmatrix}, \ x_2(0) = \begin{bmatrix} -1.2 \\ -0.7 \end{bmatrix}, \ x_3(0) = \begin{bmatrix} 0 \\ 0.2 \end{bmatrix}, \ x_4(0) = \begin{bmatrix} 1.6 \\ 0.3 \end{bmatrix}.$$

In the performance function in Eq. (5),

http://dx.doi.org/10.5772/intechopen.80285

$$Q = \begin{bmatrix} 0.45 & 0 \\ 0 & 0.3 \end{bmatrix}$$

are given. A directed interaction topology G is given in **Figure 1**, where the weights of edges of the interaction topology are 1 and the Laplacian matrix of G is

$$L = \begin{bmatrix} 1 & 0 & 0 & -1 \\ -1 & 2 & 0 & -1 \\ 0 & -1 & 1 & 0 \\ -1 & 0 & 0 & 1 \end{bmatrix}$$

By the definition of the matrix H, it is obtained that

$$H = \begin{bmatrix} 1 & -1 & 0 & 0 \\ 0 & 1 & -1 & 0 \\ 0 & 0 & 1 & -1 \end{bmatrix}.$$

Then, the matrix

$$U = \begin{bmatrix} 1 & 1 & 1 \\ -1 & 1 & 1 \\ 0 & -1 & 0 \\ -1 & -1 & -1 \end{bmatrix}$$

and $\min\{\mathrm{Re}(\lambda(HU))\} = 1$ satisfy the conditions of Lemma 2. In this simulation, $\gamma = 1.6$ is chosen. By Lemma 3 and LMI Toolbox of MATLAB, the matrix

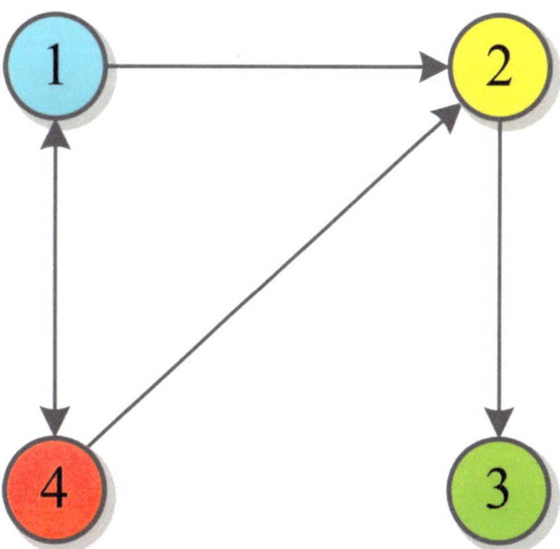

Figure 1. The interaction topology G.

$$W = \begin{bmatrix} 1.0433 & 0.0812 & -0.4787 \\ 0.0812 & 0.4320 & 0.1325 \\ -0.4787 & 0.1325 & 0.9919 \end{bmatrix}.$$

Thus, according to Theorem 3, one has

$$\tilde{P} = \begin{bmatrix} 0.5534 & -0.0481 \\ -0.0481 & 0.7672 \end{bmatrix}$$

and

$$K = [0.1139 \;\; 1.3105].$$

In **Figures 2** and **3**, the state trajectories of the nonlinear multi-agent system are shown, and one can see that the state of all agents is convergent. By Theorem 3, an upper bound of the guaranteed performance function is $J_C^* = 7.8284$. **Figure 4** presents the guaranteed performance function and the upper bound. From **Figure 3**, one can see that there exists conservatism induced by the approach taken to compute the upper bound on the performance, where the actual performance J_T and then the conservatism can be depicted by $\Delta J = J_C^* - J_T$. It is clear

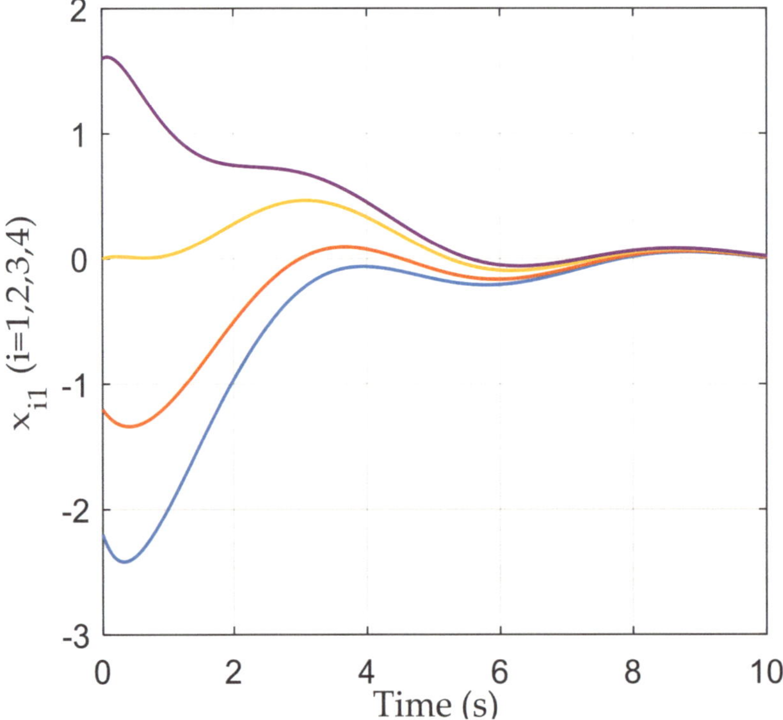

Figure 2. State trajectories of $x_{i1}(t)$ $(i = 1, 2, 3, 4)$.

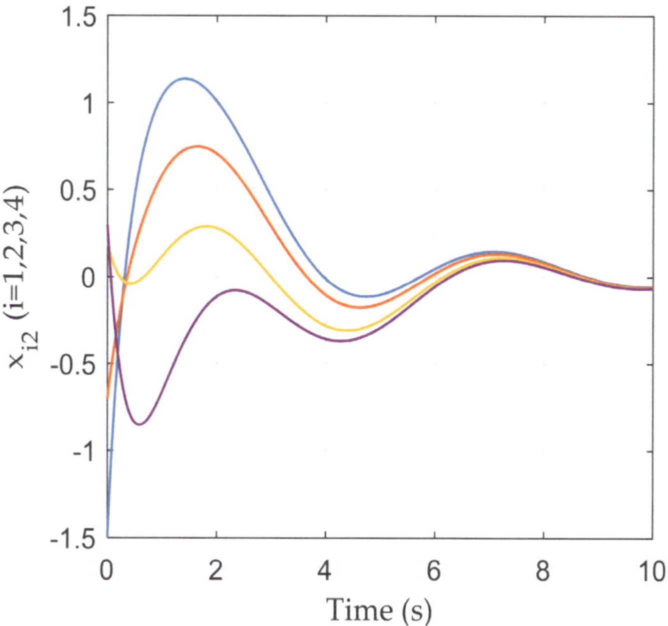

Figure 3. State trajectories of $x_{i2}(t)$ $(i = 1, 2, 3, 4)$.

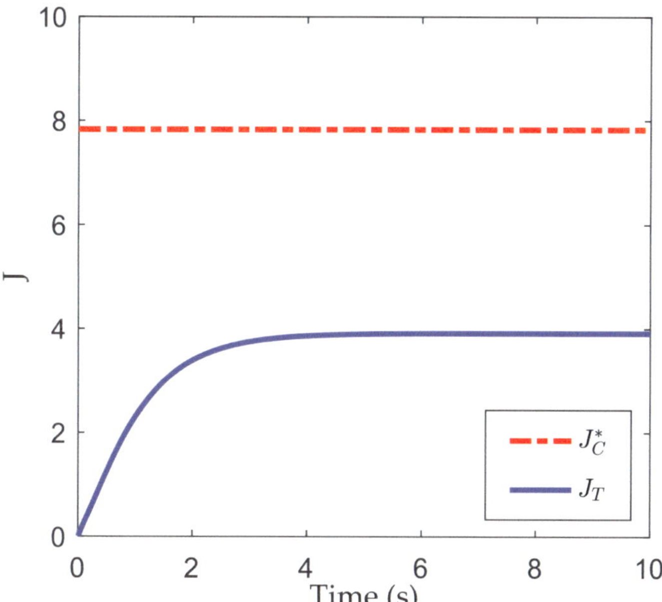

Figure 4. Trajectories of the performance function.

that the multi-agent system achieves guaranteed performance consensus although there exists conservatism.

6. Conclusions

In this chapter, the guaranteed performance consensus problems for nonlinear multi-agent systems with directed interaction topologies were studied. A special matrix transformation was introduced, and guaranteed performance consensus problems were transferred into guaranteed performance stabilization problems. Sufficient conditions for guaranteed performance consensus control were obtained, and an upper bound was given.

The directed topology was assumed to be fixed and connected in the guaranteed performance consensus problem, and then the application of conclusions of the current paper is limited. Therefore, the influence of the general switching topologies for the guaranteed performance consensus problem is the possible topic. The existing work [24, 25] assumed that the switching topologies were strongly connected and balanced, but the joint-connected switching topology cases have not been studied.

The analysis method was used to analyze the guaranteed performance consensus problem with Lipschitz-type nonlinearities in the chapter, but this method cannot be directly applied to the problem with the other kind of nonlinearities. Therefore, the analysis approach for the guaranteed performance consensus problem with general nonlinear dynamic should be given in future works.

Sliding mode control (SMC) technique has a strong robustness for external noises, such as [26, 27], and then the SMC technique is a possible method for guaranteed performance consensus problems to improve the robustness of the obtained consensus controller in future works.

Moreover, it is usually desirable to design a controller which not only achieves formation but also ensures an adequate level of performance in many practical formation control problems. Then, the idea of guaranteed performance control can be introduced into formation control problems for multi-agent systems. To this end, the guaranteed performance consensus algorithm is an effective approach, such as the guaranteed performance formation control in [28].

Acknowledgements

This work was supported by the National Natural Science Foundation of China under Grant Numbers 61703411 and 61374054 and by the Youth Foundation of High-Tech Institute of Xi'an under Grant Number 2016QNJJ004. The authors would like to thank Jianxiang Xi and Tang Zheng for providing numerical analysis and simulation.

Conflict of interest

No potential conflict of interest was reported by the authors.

Author details

Zhong Wang

Address all correspondence to: jesse.ronald@hotmail.com

High-Tech Institute of Xi'an, Xi'an, China

References

[1] Oh KK, Ahn HS. Formation control of mobile agents based on distributed position estimation. IEEE Transactions on Automatic Control. 2013;**58**(3):737-742

[2] He JP, Li H, Chen JM, Cheng P. Study of consensus-based time synchronization in wireless sensor networks. ISA Transactions. 2014;**53**(2):347-357

[3] Li ZW, Zang CZ, Zeng P, Yu HB, Li HP. MAS based distributed automatic generation control for cyber-physical microgrid system. IEEE/CAA Journal of Automatica Sinica. 2016;**3**(1):78-89

[4] Yu JJ, SM LV, Liberzon D. Rendezvous without coordinates. IEEE Transactions on Automatic Control. 2012;**57**(2):421-434

[5] Sun YZ, Wang YJ, Zhao HD. Flocking of multi-agent systems with multiplicative and independent measurement noises. Physica A: Statistical Mechanics and its Applications. 2015;**440**:81-89

[6] Olfati-Saber R, Murray RM. Consensus problems in networks of agents with switching topology and time-delays. IEEE Transactions on Automatic Control. 2004;**49**(9):1520-1533

[7] Xu YJ, Tian YP. A survey of linear and nonlinear consensus problems in multi-agent systems. Control Theory & Applications. 2014;**31**(7):837-849

[8] Cao YC, Yu W, Ren W, Chen GR. An overview of recent progress in the study of distributed multi-agent coordination. IEEE Transactions on Industrial Informatics. 2013;**9**(1):427-438

[9] Chen Y, Lü J, Yu X, Hill DJ. Multi-agent systems with dynamical topologies: Consensus and applications. IEEE Circuits and Systems Magazine. 2013;**13**(3):21-34

[10] Ren W, Beard RW, Atkins EM. Information consensus in multivehicle cooperative control. IEEE Control Systems Magazine. 2007;**27**(2):71-82

[11] Wang Z, Xi J, Yao Z, Liu G. Guaranteed cost consensus for multi-agent systems with fixed topologies. Asian Journal of Control. 2015;**17**(2):729-735

[12] Wang Z, Xi J, Yao Z, Liu G. Guaranteed cost consensus problems for second-order multi-agent systems. IET Control Theory and Applications. 2015;**9**(3):367-373

[13] Yang X, Xi J, Wu J, Yao Z. Guaranteed-cost consensus control for high-order linear swarm systems. Asian Journal of Control. 2016;**18**(2):562-568

[14] Wang Z, He M, Zheng T, Fan Z, Liu G. Guaranteed cost consensus for high-dimensional multi-agent systems with time-varying delays. IEEE/CAA Journal of Automatica Sinica. 2018;**5**(1):181-189

[15] Xi J, Yang X, Yu Z, Liu G. Leader-follower guaranteed-cost consensualization for high-order linear swarm systems with switching topologies. Journal of the Franklin Institute. 2015;**352**(4):1343-1363

[16] Zhao Y, Zhang W. Guaranteed cost consensus protocol design for linear multi-agent systems with sampled-data information: An input delay approach. ISA Transactions. 2017;**67**: 87-97

[17] Xie C, Yang G. Cooperative guaranteed cost fault-tolerant control for multi-agent systems with time-varying actuator faults. Neurocomputing. 2016;**214**:382-390

[18] Zhou X, Shi P, Lim CC, Yang C, Gui W. Event based guaranteed cost consensus for distributed multiagent systems. Journal of the Franklin Institute. 2015;**352**(9):3546-3563

[19] Cheng Y, Ugrinovskii V. Leader-follower tracking control with guaranteed consensus performance for interconnected systems with linear dynamic uncertain coupling. International Journal of Control. 2015;**88**(8):1633-1677

[20] Guan Z, Hu B, Chi M, Cheng X. Guaranteed performance consensus in second-order multi-agent systems with hybrid impulsive control. Automatica. 2014;**50**(9):2415-2418

[21] Godsil C, Royal G. Algebraic Graph Theory. New York: Springer-Verlag; 2001

[22] Liu W, Zhou SL, Qi Y, Wu X. Leaderless consensus of multi-agent systems with Lipschitz nonlinear dynamics and switching topologies. Neurocomputing. 2016;**173**:1322-1329

[23] Horn RA, Johnson CR. Matrix Analysis. Cambridge: Cambridge University Press; 1990

[24] Wang Z, Fan Z, Liu G. Guaranteed performance consensus problems for nonlinear multi-agent systems with directed topologies. International Journal of Control. 2018. DOI: 10.1080/00207179.2018.1467043

[25] Xi J, Fan Z, Liu H, Zheng T. Guaranteed-cost consensus for multi-agent networks with Lipschitz nonlinear dynamics and switching topologies. International Journal of Robust and Nonlinear Control. 2018;**28**(7):2841-2852

[26] Yu W, Wang H, Cheng F, Yu X, Wen G. Second-order consensus in multiagent systems via distributed sliding mode control. IEEE Transactions on Cybernetics. 2017;**47**(8):1872-1881

[27] Rao S, Ghose D. Sliding mode control-based autopilots for leaderless consensus of unmanned aerial vehicles. IEEE Transactions on Control Systems Technology. 2014;**22**(5): 1964-1972

[28] Wang Z, Liu G, Xi J, Xue B, Liu Y. Guaranteed cost formation control for multi-agent systems: Consensus approach. In: Proceedings of the 34th Chinese Control Conference; July 28–30, 2015. pp. 7309-7314

Chapter 5

Distributed Swarm Formation Using Mobile Agents

Yasushi Kambayashi, Ryotaro Oikawa and
Munehiro Takimoto

Additional information is available at the end of the chapter

http://dx.doi.org/10.5772/intechopen.81028

Abstract

This chapter presents decentralized control algorithms for composing formations of swarm robots. The robots are connected by communication networks. They initially do not have control program to compose formations. Control programs that implement our algorithm are introduced later from outside as mobile software agents. Our controlling algorithm is based on the pheromone communication of social insects such as ants. We have implemented the ant and the pheromone as mobile software agents. Ant agents control the robots. Each ant agent has partial information about the formation it is supposed to compose. The partial information consists of relative locations with neighbor robots that are cooperatively composing the formation. Once the ant agent detects an idle robot, it occupies that robot and generates the pheromone agent to attract other ant agents to the location for neighbor robots. Then the pheromone agent repeatedly migrates to other robots to diffuse attracting information. Once the pheromone agent reaches the robot with an ant agent, the ant agent migrates to the robot closest to the location pointed by the pheromone agent and then drives the robot to the location. We have implemented simulators based on our algorithm and conducted experiments to demonstrate the feasibility of our approach.

Keywords: mobile agents, formation control, multiple robots, ant colony optimization, swarm intelligence

1. Introduction

In the last two decades, we have witnessed mobile robot systems that consist of multiple robots such as robots playing soccer games. In performing a soccer task, the team would consist of robots with several roles such as defenders, midfielders, forwards, and a goalkeeper. If their roles are fixed to specific robots, they would have to always move around pursuing

a ball in order to cover their positions. On the other hand, if each robot can have different roles, the robots closest to the most convenient positions could achieve suitable roles without futile movement. Thus, the control manner based on multiple roles contributes to suppressing total execution cost and energy consumption. The control manner based on multiple roles, however, requires switching several programs on each robot depending on the circumstance shared by all the robots, which makes the implementation of the system difficult. Introducing mobile agents into multiroot systems solves this problem.

Mobile agent system achieves both of the ease of implementation and the execution efficiency. Each role is assigned to a specific mobile agent, and each agent migrates to the robot that is closest to the suitable position. The assignment of a role does not involve any physical movement. Furthermore, our model assumes that any agents on robots commit suicide as soon as they finish their tasks, and agents are supposed to migrate to idle robots rather than busy ones. Those control manners can decrease the total execution cost and energy consumption of not only a single task but also several tasks in multirobot systems. We have shown the advantages of mobile agents in robot systems for several applications. They are searching targets [1, 2], transporting objects to a designated collection area [3], clustering robots [4], and serialization of robots [5, 6].

In this chapter, we focus our attention on the formation control of multiple mobile robots. It is one of the most important issues for multiple mobile robots in many circumstances. Especially when individual robot has limited abilities and a given set of tasks requires collective actions, the formation control plays a vital role in a multirobot system. For example, robots may aggregate for coordinated search, that is, rescue, collectively transporting large objects, exploring and mapping unknown area, or maintaining formations for area defense or flocking [7]. In these formation algorithms, each robot needs to have the information about the entire formation. Practically, however, it is not common, for each robot knows the entire information. In this chapter, we propose distributed formation algorithms using mobile agents.

We assume that in a field, there is a fleet of robots that may be not only used for the specific task such as the formation but also shared by various different tasks because any mission is introduced into the fleet of robots by mobile agents through Wi-Fi network. For example, some robots may work for rescue, when other robots may work for mapping the area, and furthermore, these tasks may change dynamically and also the other ones may be idle state. Our goal is to propose methods that work well in such an environment and have high robustness that enables the entire robot system to continuously work even if some robots break down. The robots have capabilities of moving, and sensing length and angle to other robots, while they do not have a capability of sensing their absolute locations such as GPS. Thus, each robot must manage its coordinates as well as the coordinates of other robots in some way.

Our multirobot system is designed to use robot resources efficiently, that is, utilizing idle robots, cooperating with inaccurate devices that may have sensor errors and movement errors, composing arbitrary formations that can have various densities inside and continuing the task when some robots break down except for computers and communication devices. Furthermore, we also propose approaches that can compose a formation without any distortion even if some robots get to be out-of-order including the computers and communication devices, although the formation may be incomplete.

In this chapter, we present a pheromone-based approach toward the multirobot system that has no central control. In our robot control system, we have implemented ants and pheromones as mobile software agents. We call the mobile software agents that drive the mobile robot ant agents and call the other agent that provides communication means pheromone agent. Each ant agent on the robot requires only local neighbor information of the formation. Each ant agent has the information of relative positions of neighbor ant agents in the target formation and attracts the neighbor ant agents to the positions with their driving robots using pheromone agents. Pheromone agents diffuse to surrounding robots through migration. The ant agent not only attracts other ant agents but also is attracted by other ant agents. The bidirectional attraction results in settling all the ant agents with their driving robots down to the objective positions in the target formation without either knowledge of the whole shape of the formation. Since the attracted ant agent repeatedly migrates among the robots in the direction to the robot nearest to the target position, and then drives the robot to the target position, the pheromone-based approach contributes to suppressing energy consumption of the robots and decreasing the duration time for convergence.

The structure of the balance of this chapter is as follows. Section 2 gives the background and related works. Section 3 describes about the mobile software agents in general as preliminary information. We have extensively used an optimization method, namely ant colony optimization (ACO); therefore, in Section 4, we describe the ACO-inspired behaviors, which our mobile software agents have. In Section 5, we present a pheromone-based distributed formation control algorithm. Finally, we conclude our discussion in Section 6. The contents of this chapter are partially presented at the 10th Jubilee IEEE International Symposium on Applied Computational Intelligence and Informatics, the 13th European Conference on Multi-Agent Systems, and the Intelligent Systems Conference 2017. They are found in [8–11].

2. Background and related works

We have proposed a framework for controlling intelligent multiple robots using higher-order mobile agents [12–14]. The framework helps users to construct intelligent robot control software by migration of mobile agents. Since the migrating agents are of higher-order, a mobile agent can move into another agent so that it introduces a new feature or overrides a specific feature. The control software can be hierarchically assembled while they are running. Dynamically extending control software by the migration of mobile agents enables us to make base control software relatively simple and to add functionalities one by one as we know the working environment. Thus, we do not have to make the intelligent robot smart from the beginning or make the robot learn by itself. They can send intelligence later as new agents. We have implemented a team of cooperative search robots in order to show the effectiveness of our framework. At the same time, we have demonstrated that our framework contributes to energy saving of multiple robots [1, 12]. Based on this approach, our control algorithms are also based on mobile agents and therefore have effectiveness of improving system efficiency and suppressing energy consumption.

Recently, algorithms that are inspired by behaviors of social insects such as ants to communicate to each other by an indirect communication called stigmergy are becoming popular [15, 16].

Upon observing real ants' behaviors, Dorigo, Gambardella, Birattari, and Stützle found that ants exchanged information by laying down a trail of a chemical substance called pheromone so that other ants can follow the trail. They adopted this strategy, known as ant colony optimization (ACO), to solve various optimization problems such as the traveling salesman problem (TSP) [16]. Deneubourg et al. have originally formulated the biology-inspired behavioral algorithm that simulates the ant corps gathering and brood sorting behaviors [17]. Wang and Zhang proposed an ant-inspired approach along this line of research that sorts objects with multiple robots [18]. Lumer and Faiesta have improved Deneubourg's model and proposed a new simulation model that is called ant colony clustering [19]. Their method could cluster similar objects into a few groups.

Mizutani et al. have proposed and implemented pheromones in ACO as mobile agents [4]. In their system, both ants and pheromones are mobile agents. Ant agents repeatedly migrate among robots for searching free robots corresponding to objects. Once an ant agent finds a free robot, it drives that robot to form a cluster of robots. The pheromone agent is generated by the ant agent when its driving robot reaches a cluster, and repeatedly migrates among robots for guiding other ant agents to drive robots to the cluster. Shintani et al. have improved the mobile agent-based algorithm to serialize multiple robots while they are self-collected [5, 6]. Our approaches are extensions of the mobile agent-based clustering. Each agent that drives a robot is guided by the pheromone agents.

In the formation research area with which this chapter deals, many kinds of swarm controlling methods have been proposed. Behavior-based strategy defines simple behaviors or motion primitives for each robot. Balch and Arkin proposed the behavior-based motor scheme control [20]. Virtual structure considers the entire formation as a rigid body. The motion of each robot is translated from the motion of the virtual structure, which is determined by the definition of the dynamics of virtual structure. Lewis and Tan proposed one of the pioneering works of virtual-structure strategy [21]. In leader-following strategy, some robots are selected as leaders, and the other robots follow the leaders. Das et al. proposed one of the most popular control techniques using a feedback linearization control method in leader-following strategy [22].

Some methods have a limited class of shapes that they can form. Unsal and Bay proposed a formation method that forms shapes of rings and circles [23]. In this approach, robots issue beacons and instruct other robots to remain the position and keep a certain distance. Mamei et al. proposed similar method that composes a crude polygon and uses message hop count instead of a proximity sensor [24]. Kondacs proposed an approach that can form a large class of shapes that is inspired by biological agents that grow and die, and this approach can self-repair [25]. They use global and local compilation to automatically generate an agent. Stoy and Nagpal present a related approach to 3D self-assembly using self-reconfigurable modular robot, where individual modules must remain connected [26]. Although this system generates a wide variety of formations, it cannot create solid shapes because agents may block each other and create internal holes that agents cannot reach. To avoid this, they focus on scaffolds and porous shapes only. Gordan et al. proposed a method that forms arbitrary shape sharing common coordinate system [27]. The method, however, involves significant central computation. Although Rubenstein and Shen proposed a method that can self-repair, it can form only polar shapes [28].

Jimming Cheng, Winston Cheng, and Nagpal proposed a formation generation algorithm using contained gas model in which robots act like a particle in a container [7]. This method can construct almost arbitrary shapes, but it cannot compose a formation that does not have space inside the shapes such as line formation. Moreover, although it can keep suitable distance between robots, the density of the robots inside the formation cannot control, which means that it is not impossible to increase density partially intentionally. Our approach assumes that the shape of the formation is given and the motions of robots are determined by pheromone.

In our formation approach, mobile agents are main actors to compose a formation, and robots are just physical vehicles maneuvered by the mobile agents. The robots are only means where mobile agents move to the target locations in the formation. Therefore, any traditional approaches can be implemented on our mobile agent framework and obtain the effectiveness of its improving efficiency and saving energy. Furthermore, a mobile agent has no volume, so that mobile agents do not block any other mobile agents. Thus, our approaches can form not only line drawings but also arbitrary solid shapes and even formations with vacant area inside.

3. Mobile software agent

Object management group (OMG) has defined a set of common facilities of agents, which is called mobile agent system interoperability facility (MASIF). MASIF defines agents as computer programs that work for humans or organizations. If we give a unified notation of agents without restricting it to computer programs, it can be said that agents are independent subjects that can affect an environment through observing and taking actions for it [29, 30]. The subject means a human, a robot, or software that can be regarded as an individual object. Furthermore, the independency of the subject means that the subject can take actions based on its own experiments and knowledge for its circumstance. That is, agents are independent and intelligent subjects that interact with the environment utilizing their own intelligence and actions and making decisions based on the observation.

Recently, object-oriented programming becomes a dominant programming paradigm, where data representation and operations for it are abstracted, and only interfaces for the operations are given. Software agents can be considered as extended objects that have abilities to achieve some missions or tasks. Generally, the software agents have some features as follows:

- Autonomy: They can independently take actions.
- Reactivity: They can take actions along changes of the environment.
- Proactivity: They can take appropriate actions considering the context or intention.
- Learning capability: They can take actions based on knowledge and experiments.
- High-level communication: They can communicate with agents or humans through specific or natural languages.
- Cooperation: They can attain cooperation with other agents or humans.

- Character: They have names, features, or objects that are distinguished from other agents.
- Mobility: They can migrate among computer through a network.

Mobile agents are a kind of software agents but can independently and actively migrate to another computer through a network while continuing its computations. The mobility enables the agents to asynchronously perform tasks and to suppress communication costs [29, 30].

Figure 1 shows a model of mobile agent system. In the model, a mobile agent on computer 1 is able to migrate to computer 2 directly through a network and continuously execute its own tasks on computer 2.

Efficient use of network band is one of the advantages of the mobile agent model. Mobile agents are able to migrate to another computer, locally access its resources, and come back to the original computer with only the result of computations. Also, mobile agents are able to utilize information of the destination load. In intermittently communicating environments, mobile agents are able to continue their own tasks even while disconnecting the communications. We can summarize the advantages of mobile agents as follows.

Suppressing communication costs: In server-client model, communication cost often becomes high because the communication between a server and a client has to keep connection. In mobile agent model, the connections are restricted to migrations of the agents among computers. That is, the connection is not necessary after the agents migrate to another machine. This feature of mobile agents contributes to suppressing communication costs.

Suppressing network load: The connection feature of mobile agents mentioned above also contributes to suppression of network loads.

Asynchronous processing: Each mobile agent is an autonomous entity, and therefore, its behaviors follow asynchronous processing.

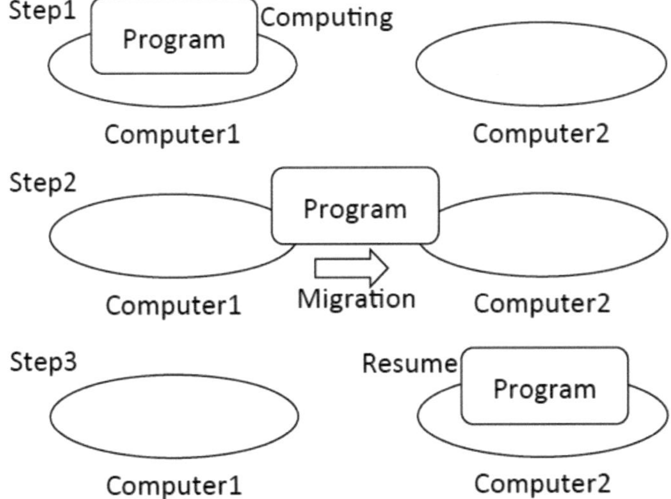

Figure 1. Mobile agent model.

Balancing loads: Each mobile agent can select the destination of migration autonomously. This means that it can contribute to load balancing, if it preferentially selects an idle machine as a destination.

An agent defined by MASIF has two kinds of states. They are (1) execution states and (2) attribute states. The execution states mean the states of context for executing any programs, such as counter or an execution stack. Attribute states are derived from the mobile agent's own data such as variables or arrays, which is decided by its mission, i.e., program. A mobile agent has to transfer not only program code but also these states to another site through migrations. This means that they have to be saved in a file as persistent data in order to transfer them to a destination site, and then, restored in loading the mobile agent's code at the destination.

Mobile agent systems often use a server system to implement their mobility. We also use server-based systems, AgentSpace and MobileSpace that were developed by Ichiro Sato. MobileSpace, which is an extension of AgentSpace, enables mobile agents to be composed hierarchically. Both systems are built using Java programming language. In Java, programs are not allowed to refer the program counter or the execution stack in a virtual machine. Thus, mobile agents implemented in Java are able to transfer only the values of their instance variables. AgentSpace and MobileSpace are middle wares for distributed computation implemented in Java language, which are free open source programs. These systems consists of an API part that makes construction of mobile agent applications easy and a run-time system part that gives services for execution and migration to mobile agents. These API and run-time system, which are shared by all the mobile agents, enable each mobile agent to be efficient and independent of the others [31]. AgentSpace and MobileSpace transfer their attribute states to the destination site with class files, but not execution sates. Some other systems also transfer execution states, which require costly process for each migration. We use AgentSpace to implement our agent-based distributed robot formation control systems.

4. ACO-inspired behavior

Our mobile agents have behavior inspired by ant colony optimization (ACO). In this section, we describe the details of the ACO-inspired behavior. A pheromone communication such as ant's route exploration can be modeled as a communication of multiagent system, for which various methods are studied. ACO is one of the most practical multiagent systems. ACO has been applied to solving a traveling salesman problem or network routing problem [32, 33]. ACO is a kind of metaheuristics that is used to obtain quasioptimal solutions independently of specific computational conditions. The metaheuristics try to resolve problems by introducing the following two notions:

Probabilistic action selection of an artificial ant agent: The random factor enables an agent not to repeat the same sequence of actions even if the same information is used. Namely, the controlling manner of agents enables agent to widely explore when the agents cannot decide which options to select, and to intensively explore when agent has confidence for which option to select.

Pheromone evaporation: This imitates the behavior of physical pheromones. Pheromones emitted by each agent evaporate over time. This prevents old information remain for a long time. Thus, the notion of pheromone evaporation keeps information fresh in ACO algorithm.

4.1. Basic concept of pheromone

In the science of ecology, pheromone is defined as chemical substance emitted by living things, which contributes to communications among the same species. For example, some pheromones attract other individuals that detect that pheromone, and some pheromones notify other individuals around them of danger. For both cases, the properties of evaporation and diffusion of pheromones are important. Evaporation contributes to decreasing older information over time. This property enables newer information to constantly be major. Diffusion contributes to expanding pheromones from their birth point to their surroundings. This property enables pheromones to propagate their information at some distance.

4.2. Pheromone communication

Ants maintain a social system by sharing some roles as if they are one individual. In the system, each individual takes actions for a whole swarm, and occasionally they devote their life to defend their swarm. Although each individual behavior seems to be randomly decided based on their judgment depending on various distributed and local factors, the whole swarm seems to suitably behave from the macroperspective. Many ants have restricted capability of sight, and in most cases, depend on the stimulus from tactile organ. Thus, they communicate not through visual information but through chemical signals sensed by the tactile organs. These signals are called pheromone and social insects such as ants communicate each other using the pheromone instead of languages or visual methods.

In ant colony, ants organize and control a swarm, using dozens of kinds of pheromones. Each individual emits a specific pheromone considering each situation. Then, distributed information through the pheromones is shared by other individual ants. Since this process is performed with time and spatial locality, it contributes to communications between individuals. Also, the shared information behaves a swarm organized by individuals as if each individual knows the optimal behaviors, so that the ant colony exhibits semioptimal behaviors.

4.3. Foraging of ants

Foraging is one of the most important tasks for worker ants to maintain their colony. The foraging process consists of exploring and transporting foods. Generally, the worker ants are divided into exploring ants and transporting ants. Once exploring ants find a food, they go back to colleagues in their nest through putting guidepost pheromone on their return path. After that, transporting ants go to the food following the guidepost pheromone using their tactile organs. Once transporting ants reach the food, they immediately catch the food and take it to their nest. At this time, transporting ants also put pheromones on their traces such as exploring ants. Although this sequence of actions seems to be simple, and indeed, the rules that each ant follows are simple. In seeing them as a swarm, however, the swarm shows a kind of intelligent behavior that seems to explore the shortest path between the nest and food.

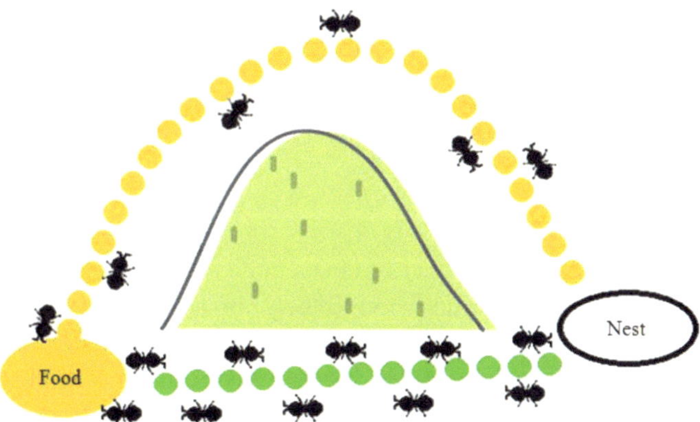

Figure 2. Ants take shorter path after initial search phase.

The observed intelligent behaviors for a swarm are collectively called swarm intelligence. For example, consider a branch path as shown in **Figure 2**. The first ant randomly selects a path at the branch. The second ant tends to select the path through which the first ant walked, because the first ant put pheromones on the path. Notice that the ants that select the shorter path reach a target earlier than the ants that select the longer path. Pheromones on the longer path evaporate earlier than pheromones in the shorter path, and then pheromones on the longer path spontaneously disappear, while pheromones in the shorter path become more stronger. As a result, the path that ants intensively select is the shortest path in high probability. Thus, strengthening phenomenon is positive feedback of route selection, which is the mechanism of ants' route selection. This mechanism achieves the optimization of detecting the shortest path without individual intelligence.

Suppose an ant *k* (in *m* ants) is at a junction *i*. Then, the ant chooses the direction to a junction *j* in a probabilistic way as follows:

$$p^k(i,j) = \frac{[\tau(i,j)]^{\alpha}[\eta(i,j)]^{\beta}}{\sum_{l \in N^k}[\tau(i,l)]^{\alpha}[\eta(i,l)]^{\beta}} \tag{1}$$

here, $\eta(i,j)$ represents the reciprocal of the distance between two junctions *i* and *j*. α and β are nonnegative constants, and their values are determined by whether one attaches importance to global information or local information. $\tau(i,j)$ represents the information added by ants, that is, the pheromone value on the route between two junctions *i* and *j*. This value is updated in the following rules, when one iteration is done.

$$\tau(i,j) \leftarrow (1-\rho)\tau(i,j) + \sum_{k=1}^{m}\Delta\tau^k(i,j) \tag{2}$$

$$\Delta\tau^k(i,j) = \begin{cases} 1/L^k & if(i,j) \in T^k \\ 0 & \text{otherwise} \end{cases} \tag{3}$$

here, T^k represents the set of all routes from source to destination, and L^k represents the collective distance from source to destination. In ACO algorithms, the pheromone value added to a specific route is determined by the reciprocal of the total distance and the pheromone also disappears over time, where ρ represents the evaporation rate so that newly added pheromone has more influence than old pheromone additions. Thus, after many of iterations, one can expect to obtain quasioptimal route from the nest to the location of food.

4.4. Ants as multiagent system

As mentioned above, there are no supervisors that lead a whole swarm in ant colony systems. Although a queen ant is central character in a colony, the queen ant does not control worker ants and an individual worker ant that has multiple roles takes actions based on its locally perceiving information. On the other hand, a colony constantly maintains the state of ant colony system in certain quality as a whole.

In other words, each individual takes actions based on local action rules, changing the environment using pheromones, which accomplish route exploration indirectly. The notion of communication through mutual interactions based on the change of an environment is called stigmergy in ethology. This word, which roots from stigma (means sign) and ergon (means work), means obtaining a next action sign from work. That is, stigmergy is an indirect communication that tunes cooperative operation among individuals. In ant colony, the process where ants emit pheromone based on perceived local information and other ants perceive it feedback the change of an environment around ants to the ants, so that it enables the ants to adapt to complicated situations. **Figure 3** shows the system of ants as multiagents.

The generality and flexibility of ant colony are often applied to the design of artificial systems. The systems are called multiagent systems, which are actively studied in fields such as artificial intelligence, artificial life, robots engineering, and other various computer science fields. Certainly, our distributed formation control system is a typical multiagent system.

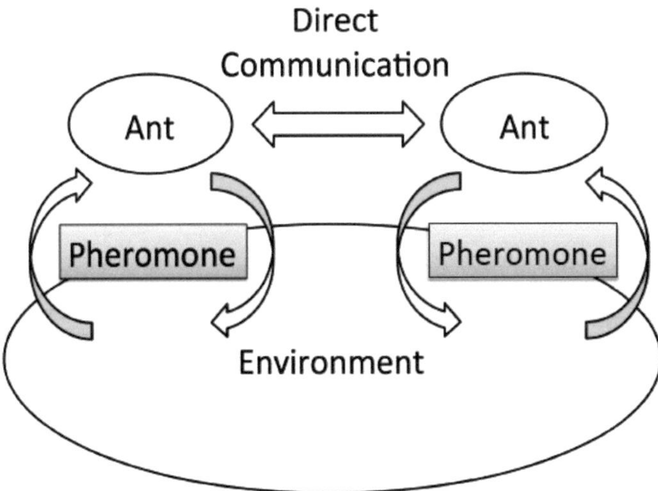

Figure 3. Ant as multiagent.

http://dx.doi.org/10.5772/intechopen.81028

5. Pheromone-based formation

In this section, we present a decentralized control algorithm to compose any formations of mobile swarm robots. In this approach, mobile agents imitate pheromone communication of ants. The swarm robots are expected to compose any formations. The robots are connected by communication networks and not necessary intelligent; they initially do not have any control program to compose formations. Control programs that implement our algorithm are introduced later from outside as mobile software agents, which are able to migrate from one robot to another robot connected by the network. Our controlling algorithm is based on the indirect pheromone communication of social insects, that is, ants. We have implemented the ant and the pheromone as mobile software agents. Each ant agent has partial information about the formation and drives a robot based on the information to compose the formation. The partial information consists of relative locations of neighbor robots to cooperatively compose the target formation. Once the ant agent detects an idle robot, it occupies that robot and generates the pheromone agent to attract the specific ant agents to the location with neighbor robots. The pheromone agent repeatedly migrates to other robots to diffuse attracting information. Once the pheromone agent reaches the robot with an ant agent, the ant agent migrates to the robot closest to the location pointed by the pheromone agent, and then, drives the robot to the location. We have implemented a simulator based on our algorithm and conducted experiments to demonstrate the feasibility of our approach.

5.1. System overview

Our system consists of robots and two kinds of mobile software agents. We assume that the robots have simple capabilities of movement such as rolling wheels, measuring distance, and angle through an optical camera and other sensors. In addition to the mobile capability, the robots have some communication devices with which they can communicate each other through a communication network such as a wireless LAN.

All the controls for the mobile robots are achieved through the mobile agents. They are ant agents (AAs) and pheromone agents (PAs). In our algorithm, AAs attract each other to suitable positions as in **Figure 4** without any central coordinate that directs the other robots to compose a formation. In this figure, robots are represented as circles, and the neighbor locations of each robot are represented as stars to which vectors relative to the robot point, where vectors are represented as black arrows. The neighbor locations are supposed to be occupied by other robots to compose the formation. Colored arrows represent attracting force by pheromone. We assume that the target formations are represented as a set of positions of robots. For example, a line formation F_{line} whose length is 30 is represented by four robots such as $F_{line} = \{(0, 0), (0, 10), (0, 20), (0, 30)\}$.

Each AA takes charge of one position in a formation and drives a robot to the position. We assume that all the AAs are sent from the outside user machine to one of the reachable robots, and each AA does not know its own absolute position but has partial information of the formation. For example, when the target formation is a circle and AA *A*'s neighbors are B and *C* as shown **Figure 5**, *A* has only information of *B* and *C* represented as colored arrows in the figure ($\boldsymbol{P}_{AB}$ and $\boldsymbol{P}_{AC}$).

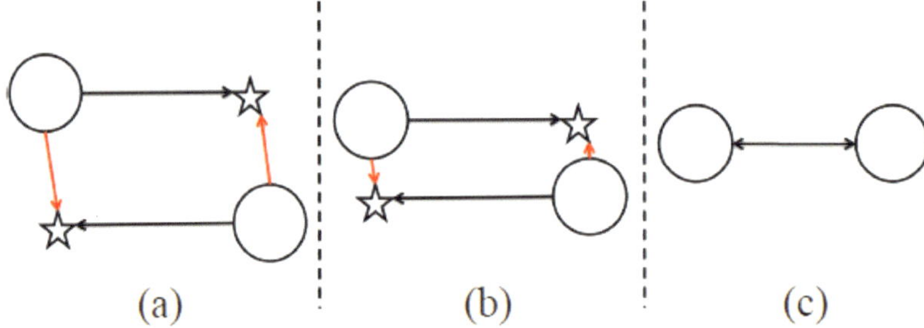

Figure 4. The process of composing a formation.

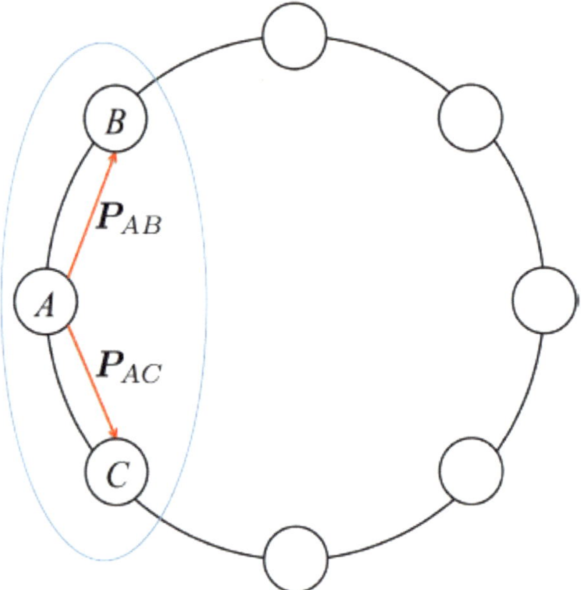

Figure 5. Local shape information of the ant agent *A*.

For simplicity, we assume that each robot can obtain a common direction by using devices such as compass. Each robot can measure an angle to another robot based on that common direction. We assume that when an agent that was on robot *A* migrates to robot *B*, robot *B* has a different coordinate (direction) from *A*'s as shown in **Figure 6**. As shown in the figure, θ_A is the angle to robot *B* from robot *A* and θ_B is to *A* from *B*, and dotted arrows represent robot's angles. When the agent on *A* migrates to *B*, the agent translates all the vector data it has such as the target location vector to adjust to *B*'s coordinate. To do this, we calculate the difference θ_r of angles between the two robots as follows:

$$\theta_r = 180 - (\theta_B - \theta_A) \tag{4}$$

In other words, the agent rotates its data vectors that are based on *A*'s coordinate by the difference angle θ_r.

http://dx.doi.org/10.5772/intechopen.81028

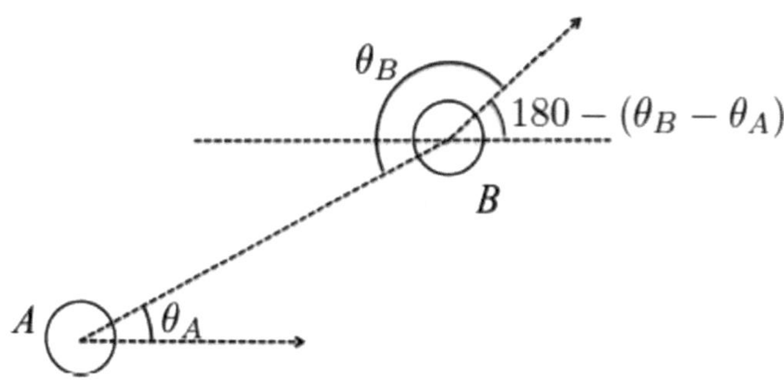

Figure 6. Rotation angle.

5.2. Ant agent

In this section, we describe the algorithm for AAs (Algorithm 1). AAs can migrate to robots through communication network. First, AAs traverse robots scattered in the field one by one to search idle robots. Once an AA finds an idle robot, the AA occupies that robot and generates PAs. The PA has vector values that point to the positions of neighbor AAs to compose the formation. The positions of neighbor AAs mean the positions of robots to compose the given formation. Neighbor AAs are supposed to drive robots to those positions. As long as an AA resides on an idle robot, it generates PAs at some intervals, which migrate to other robots to diffuse the information for attraction. Each PA has data V_t from the attractee to the neighbor location of its attractor. Once AA corresponding to the attractee receives the PA, the AA migrates to the robot closest to the objective location guided by the PA and then drives that robot to the location. If an AA simultaneously receives n PAs with vector V_i, vector V_t held by the AA is computed as follows.

$$V_t = \frac{1}{n}\sum_{i=1}^{n} V_i \tag{5}$$

Algorithm 1 Ant Agents' behavior

```
if Current robot is idle then
  Generate PAs
  if The AA received PAs from other AAs then
    Synthesize vectors from PAs and directions
    Move to the synthesized location or migrate to a neighbor robot
  end if
else
  Migrate to another robot through network
end if
```

For example, the objective formation is a line with three robots, which are currently located as shown in **Figure 7**. In this figure, the stars represent the positions for AAs to occupy and are eventually the positions occupied by the robots. AA A is supposed to drive one robot to its corresponding position, and colored arrows represent vectors to the positions. A synthesizes

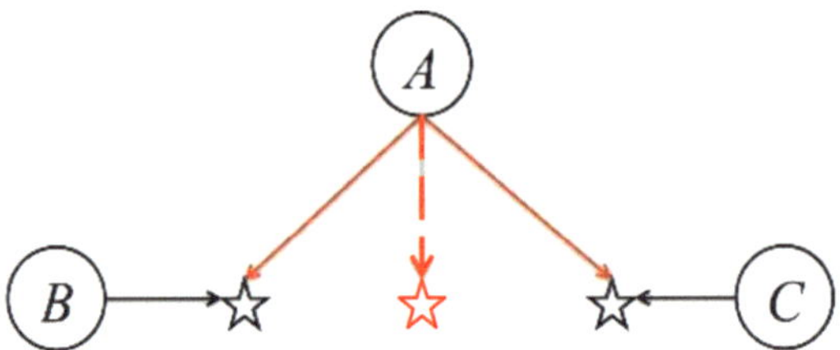

Figure 7. An example of vector synthesis.

the two vectors, resulting in new vector represented by the dashed arrow. The colored star is the position to where AA A must physically drive the robot. Once the AA finds some other robots within the view range, the AA judges whether to migrate to one of them by comparing $\boldsymbol{V}_t$ with the vector $\boldsymbol{V}_{another-to-dst}$ from the another robot to the destination, which is computed by using vector $\boldsymbol{V}_{another}$ to the another robot as follows:

$$\boldsymbol{V}_{another\text{-}to\text{-}dst} = \boldsymbol{V}_t - \boldsymbol{V}_{another} \tag{6}$$

If another robot is idle and $|\boldsymbol{V}_t|/2 > |\boldsymbol{V}_{another-to-dst}|$, the AA migrates to it instead of driving the current robot along $\boldsymbol{V}_t$. Notice that all the AAs are attracted each other along the guidance of PAs, so that they may be attracted with the total strength of them. This means that if an AA migrates to another robot when $|\boldsymbol{V}_t| > |\boldsymbol{V}_{another-to-dst}|$, the robot could overrun, so that it may waste extra time for convergence. The conditional migration of AA enables it to move to a robot closer to the destination without physically driving its current robot, which decreases not only convergence time but also the total energy consumption. Thus, the vector values play important roles in our system. In an absolute coordinate system, it is easy to compare or synthesize them. Each AA has, however, only an individual relative coordinate system. Therefore, PAs store angle values of coordinate system of the attractor AA that generated them and the attractee AA receiving the PAs adjusts its coordinate system by using angle values of them. Let θ be the angle value that the AA has, n be the number of the PAs that the AA receives, and θ_i be an angle value that ith PA has. Once an AA receives a series of PAs with those angle values, the AA updates its angle value as follows:

$$\theta = \frac{1}{n+1}\left(\theta + \sum_{i=1}^{n} \theta_i\right) \tag{7}$$

In this manner, all the individual coordinate systems are averaged and AA's driving direction converges to a certain angle. Therefore, the final location and the direction of the formation depend on the initial locations of the robots and the initial angles of the AAs.

5.3. Pheromone agent

In this section, we describe the algorithm for PAs (Algorithm 2). Each PA is responsible for guiding the specific AA to the location to occupy in the formation. A PA generated by an attractor AA seeks its attractee AA by traversing robots. Once the PA finds the attractee AA, the PA repeats the following behaviors (**Figure 8**):

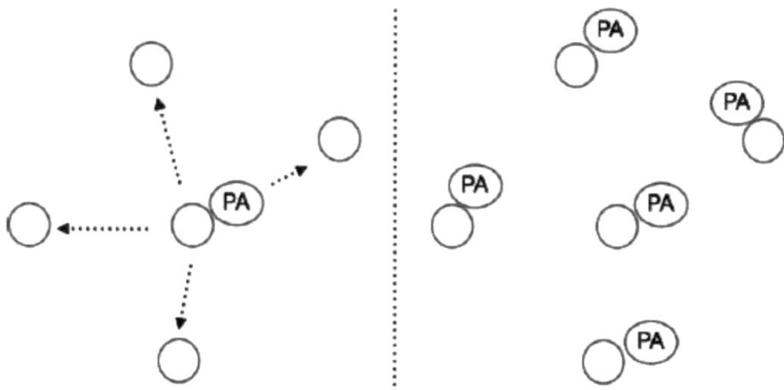

Figure 8. PAs clone themselves and migrate to neighbor robots.

1. PAs clone themselves on the current robots.
2. PAs migrate to all the other robots within the view range of the current robots.

Algorithm 2 Pheromone Agents' behavior

```
if Current robot has an AA then
    if The AA isn't one of attractees of this PA then
        Clone itself and migrate to neighbor robots
    else
        Stop migration
    end if
else
    Clone itself and migrate to neighbor robots
end if
if Certain time has passed from when generating then
    Defuse itself
end if
```

Since PAs are repeatedly generated on the same attractor AA, some of them may reach the same attractee AA through different routes at the same time. In this case, the attractee AA picks up the last PA and discards the other ones, in order to follow the latest information. Also, each PA has "time to live" and fades away after a certain time has elapsed as real pheromones evaporate, so that the information diffused by PAs is kept fresh. The information of PAs includes identifiers of the attractor and attractee AAs and a vector value pointing to the neighbor location of the attractor. The attractor AA's id is used to check if the current robot is already engaged in a destination to reach. The vector value has to be updated so that it keeps on pointing to the same location, whenever the PA migrates to another robot. The current vector V_t is updated using vector V_n to the destination robot of the migration as follows:

$$V_t \leftarrow V_t - V_n \tag{8}$$

Figure 9 shows an example process where a PA updates V_t along with the migration path (A, B, C, D). Initially, the PA is on robot A and V_t points to the location to occupy

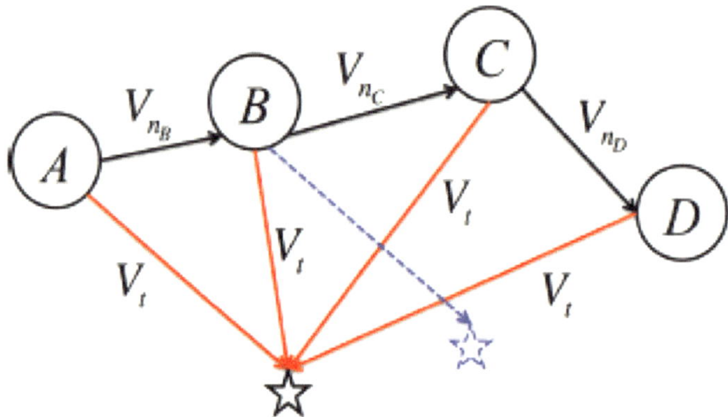

Figure 9. PAs update a target vector when PAs migrate.

represented by the solid line star. Once it migrates to robot *B*, V_t would point to the location represented by the dotted line star. In order to make V_t keep pointing to the black star, the PA has to adjust V_t through the calculation: $V_t \leftarrow V_t - V_{nB}$, where V_{nB} is the vector to robot *B* from robot *A*. In the same manner, the PA repeats adjustments of V_t on robot *B*, *C*, and *D*, so that V_t still points to the black star on robot *D*.

5.4. Experimental results

In order to demonstrate the correctness and effectiveness of our method, we have implemented a simulator and conducted numerical experiments on it. In the experiments, we assume the following conditions.

- Robots are randomly placed in an 800 × 800 square field in the simulator.
- The reachable range of Wi-Fi network for each robot is 150 units.
- Each robot can move 2 units in each step in the simulator.
- Interval time of generating PAs is 1 step.
- Duration time of PAs is 10 steps.
- The initial locations and angles of robots are randomly determined without overlapping.
- Each robot is represented as a circle on the grid field.
- Robots that have an AA are emphasized by large circle.

We confirmed that robots converge to the target formation as shown in **Figure 10** where the location and angle of the formation is determined by an initial condition. **Figure 11** shows the result of the formation that represents the letter A in different initial conditions from **Figure 10**. As shown in the figures, the initial conditions determine the location and the angle of the resulted formation.

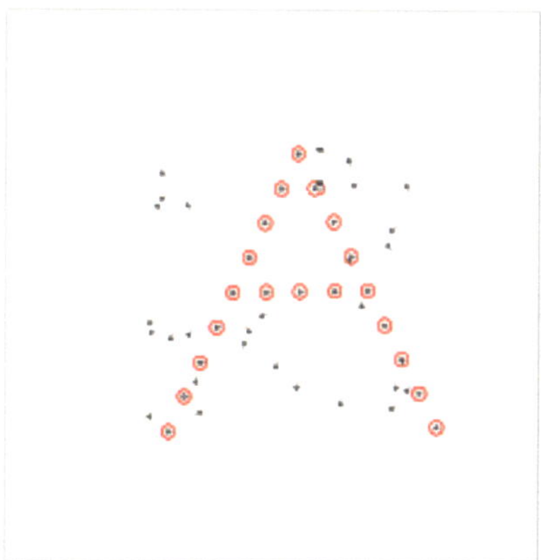

Figure 10. Formation of letter A.

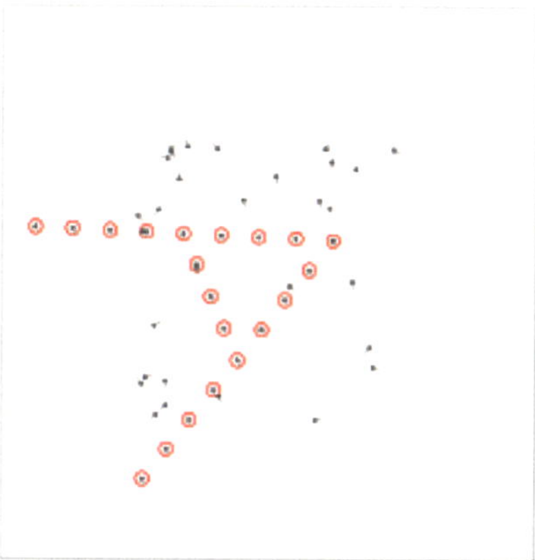

Figure 11. Formation of letter A (2).

Migrations to other robots contribute to reducing the time for convergence and the total length of movements of robots. We have measured the convergence time for the different numbers of robots between 20 and 50 with the interval 10. The objective shape is a circle whose radius is 150 units, and it consists of 20 robots.

When the number of robots is 20, all the robots must participate in the formation, and there is not any idle robot. On the other hand, when we increased the number of robots to 50, AAs can use extra 30 idle robots for migration. In order to measure quantitatively the degree of correspondence with the objective ideal formation, we calculated the average distance D as defined in Eq. (9). We calculated the barycenter for both actual and ideal points, calculating all relative coordinate of robots from the barycenter. Then, we average all the distances between actual and ideal relative coordinates $\boldsymbol{A}_i$ and $\boldsymbol{I}_i$, calculating the average distance D by the following equation:

$$\mathrm{D} = \frac{1}{n}\sum_{i=1}^{n}\|\boldsymbol{I}_i - \boldsymbol{A}_i\| \tag{9}$$

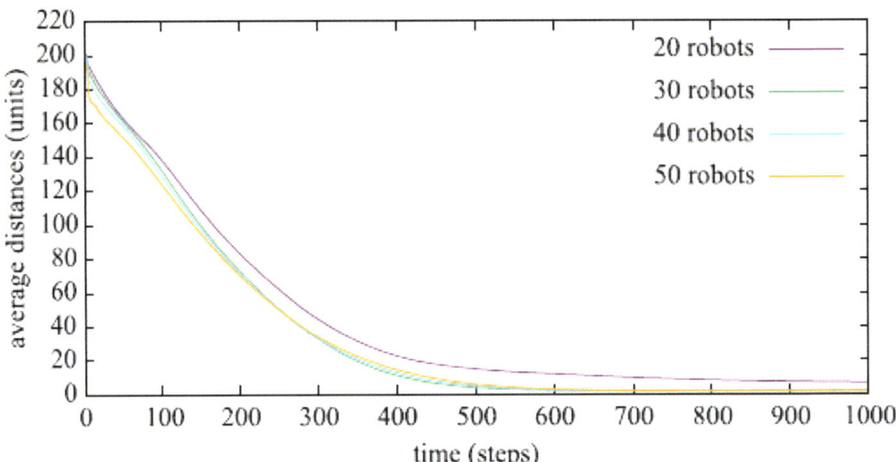

Figure 12. Time for convergence for the different number of robots.

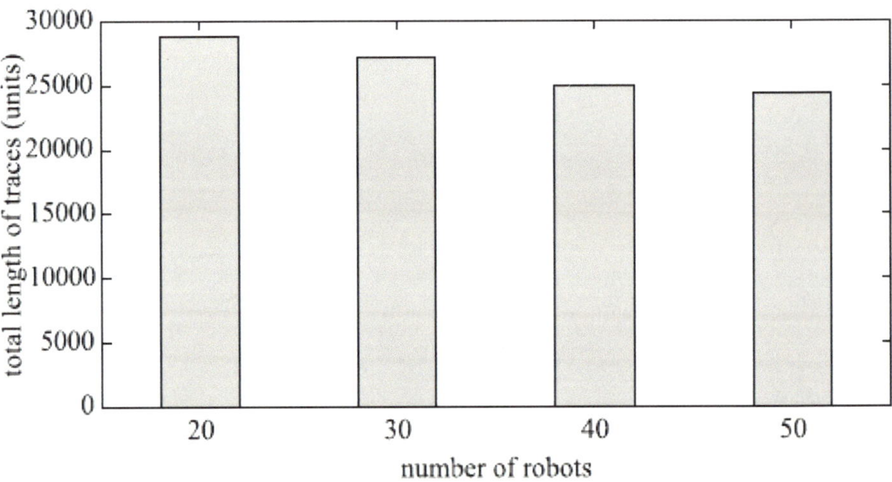

Figure 13. Total length of movements for different number of robots.

I_i is the ideal relative coordinate of the ith robot from the barycenter and A_i is the actual relative coordinate of ith robot from the barycenter. In the equation, n is the number of AAs that compose a given shape. **Figures 12** and **13** show the processes of convergence and the total length of movements until the time steps 1000. The horizontal axes are the duration time and the numbers of robots, respectively, and the vertical axes are the average distance from actual AAs' current locations to the ideal locations in the formation and total length of movements of all the robots with AAs, respectively. As shown in **Figure 12**, the migration can reduce the duration time for convergence, and if the number of idle robots is more than enough, which is over 10, the measures of duration time for convergence are almost identical. Also, as shown in **Figure 13**, if the number of robots is more than enough, the extra idle robots can contribute to reducing the total length of movements of robots. To show the effectiveness of migration from

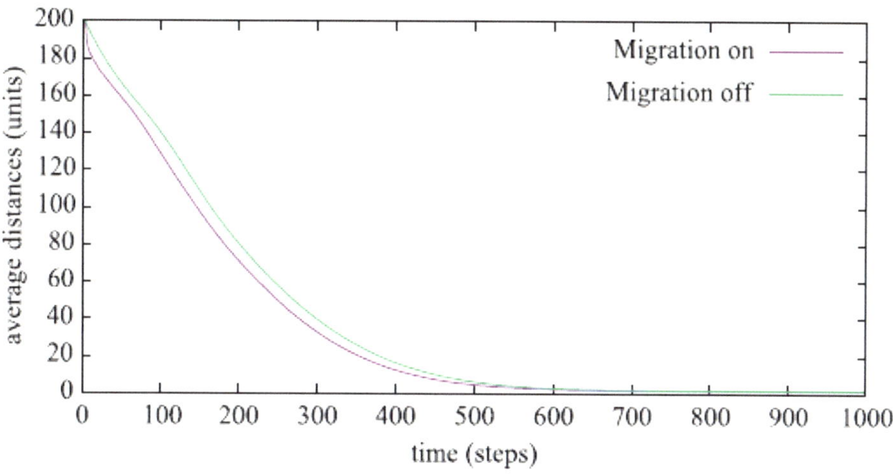

Figure 14. Time for convergence compared to migration off.

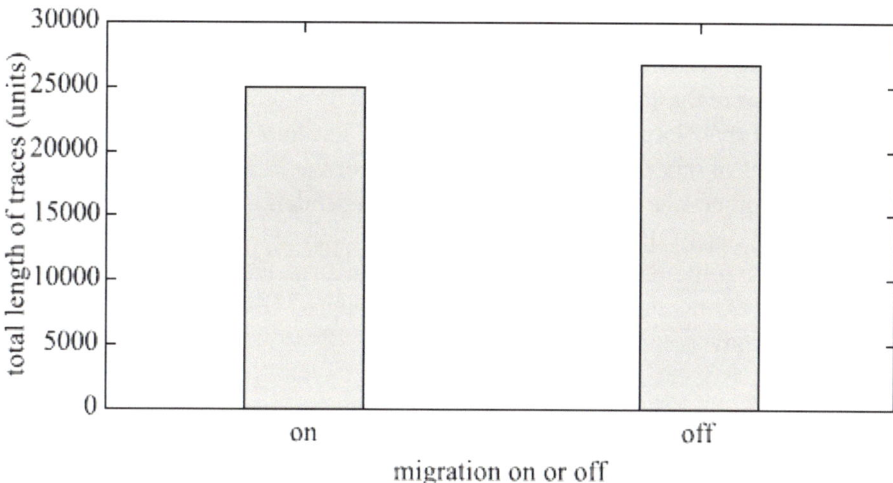

Figure 15. Total length of movements compared to migration off.

another aspect, we fixed the number of robots to 40. Under such a condition, we measured the duration time for convergence and length of movements and compared with those with no migration. As shown in **Figures 14** and **15**, the time for convergence and total length of movements were reduced by the migration.

We have examined the relation between the duration time for convergence and the number of AAs composing the formation, where we fixed the target formation to a circle with the radius of 150 and set the number of robots to 40, and under this condition, we changed the number of AAs composing the formation to 10, 20, and 30. The reason why we set the number of robots to 40 is that 10 extra idle robots are just enough to take advantage of migration as shown in **Figure 12**. **Figure 16** shows that the duration time for convergence increases as the

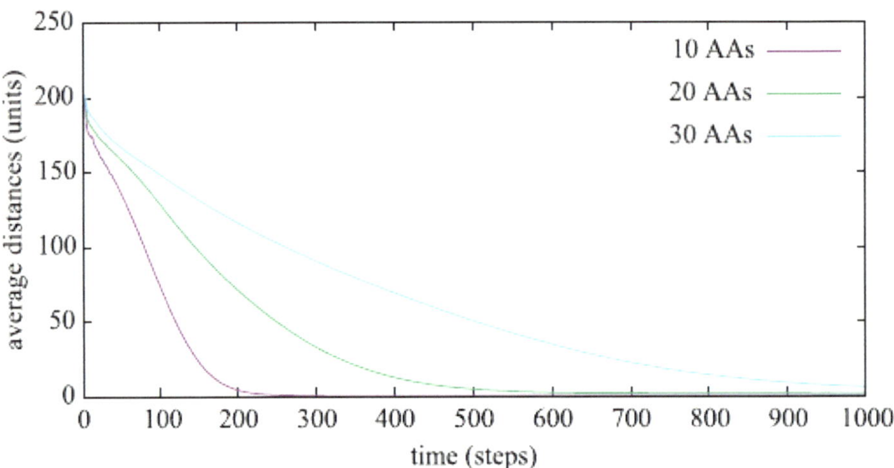

Figure 16. Time for convergence for different number of AAs.

number of AAs increases. In our algorithm, the location of formation is determined by the initial locations of robots. Once one AA moves to compose a formation, the whole formation is affected. The change of the location of an AA is observed by neighbor AAs and then the neighboring AAs adjust their locations. The changes of the locations of the neighbor AAs cause further adjustments of others. In this way, the change of the location of an AA is repeatedly propagated to the other AAs. At this time, for mutual-dependence relation, reverse directional propagation is also caused. Eventually, the whole formation settles down to a certain location after oscillation for some time. Thus, we can expect that as the target formations become larger, the number of time steps for propagating the changes of locations increases, so that the duration time for convergence also increases.

6. Conclusions and future works

In this chapter, we presented formation control methods based on mobile software agents that have the following features: (1) it does not have central computation; (2) it can efficiently use robot resources; (3) it can reconcile with sensor errors or movement errors; (4) it makes swarm robots compose arbitrary formations with various density inside the formations; and (5) it let swarm robots continue the task when some of them break down except for computers and communication devices because mobile agent can migrate other unbroken robots.

Our approaches make accurately arrange mobile robots to the proper places in a given formation. Upon composing the formation, each robot is not reserved for a specific position in the formation. Instead, each mobile agent is reserved for the position. This means that the mobile agent-based control manner simulates a system where each robot has a specific role in distributed environments, although any robot does not actually have its own role. The property of our approaches enables users to easily implement sophisticated formation without sacrificing scalability and robustness as a distributed system.

In order to implement our approach, we have used decentralized algorithms for the formation control for swarm robots using mobile agents. In the algorithm, we introduced two kinds of mobile software agents; that is, ant agents and pheromone agents. Ant agents generate pheromone agents that have local information about the formation to guide other ant agents to the appropriate locations to form the target formation. Once pheromone agents are generated, pheromone agents clone themselves and migrate to other robots to find target ant agents. When ant agents receive pheromone agents, which have information to guide the ant agents, the ant agents move to the locations that the pheromone agents point to. Eventually the whole robots compose the target formation. In order to show the feasibility of our algorithm, we have implemented a simulator on which we have conducted numerical experiments. We have shown that the algorithm can achieve not only the distributed formation control but also suppressing energy consumption through the experiments.

Our approach can continue tasks when robots get in trouble and cannot move, because even from the troubled robots, ant agents can migrate to other trouble-free robots. Once ant agents are lost, however, our current approaches cannot complete the formation. As a future work, we will give a solution to address this problem. For example, since the pheromone-based approach can compose a formation with some lacks of robots, ant agents corresponding to the lost positions could also be recognized by their neighbor ant agents through observing the pheromone agents to attract the lost ones. At this time, the neighbor agents could create new ant agents for the lost positions.

Acknowledgements

This work is partially supported by Japan Society for Promotion of Science (JSPS), with the basic research program (C) (No. 26350456, 26750076 and 17K01304), Grant-in-Aid for Scientific Research (KAKENHI), and Suzuki Foundation.

Author details

Yasushi Kambayashi[1]*, Ryotaro Oikawa[2] and Munehiro Takimoto[2]

*Address all correspondence to: yasushi@nit.ac.jp

1 Nippon Institute of Technology, Miyashiro, Japan

2 Tokyo University of Science, Noda, Japan

References

[1] Nagata T, Takimoto M, Kambayashi Y. Cooperatively searching objects based on mobile agents. In: Transaction on Computational Collective Intelligence XI, Vol. 8065 of Lecture Notes in Computer Science. 2013. pp. 119-136

[2] Abe T, Takimoto M, Kambayashi Y. Searching targets using mobile agents in a large scale multi-robot environment. In: Proceedings of the First KES International Symposium

on Agent and Multi-Agent Systems (KES-AMSTA 2011), Vol. 6682 of Lecture Notes in Artificial Intelligence. 2011. pp. 211-220

[3] Shibuya R, Takimoto M, Kambayashi Y. Suppressing energy consumption of transportation robots using mobile agents. In: Proceedings of the 5th International Conference on Agents and Artificial Intelligence (ICAART 2013). SciTePress; 2013. pp. 219-224

[4] Mizutani M, Takimoto M, Kambayashi Y. Ant colony clustering using mobile agents as ants and pheromone. In: Proceedings of the Second Asian Conference on Intelligent Information and Database Systems Applications of Intelligent Systems (ACIDS 2010), Lecture Notes in Computer Science 5990. Springer-Verlag; 2010. pp. 435-444

[5] Shintani M, Lee S, Takimoto M, Kambayashi Y. Synthesizing pheromone agents for serialization in the distributed ant colony clustering. In: ECTA and FCTA 2011—Proceedings of the International Conference on Evolutionary Computation Theory and Applications and the Proceedings of the International Conference on Fuzzy Computation Theory and Applications [Parts of the International Joint Conference on Computational Intelligence (IJCCI 2011)]. SciTePress; 2011. pp. 220-226

[6] Shintani M, Lee S, Takimoto M, Kambayashi Y. A serialization algorithm for mobile robots using mobile agents with distributed ant colony clustering. In: Knowledge-Based and Intelligent Information and Engineering Systems, Vol. 6881 of Lecture Notes in Computer Science. Berlin, Heidelberg: Springer; 2011. pp. 260-270

[7] Cheng J, Cheng W, Nagpal R. Robust and self-repairing formation control for swarms of mobile agents. In: AAAI'05 Proceedings of the 20th National Conference on Artificial Intelligence. Vol. 1. AAAI Press; 2005. pp. 59-64

[8] Oikawa R, Takimoto M, Kambayashi Y. Distributed formation control for swarm robots using mobile agents. In: Proceedings of the Tenth Jubilee IEEE International Symposium on Applied Computational Intelligence and Informatics. 2015. pp. 111-116

[9] Oikawa R, Takimoto M, Kambayashi Y. Predictive distributed formation control for swarm robots using Mobile agents. Transactions on Automatic Control and Computer Science. 2016;**61**(1):83-90

[10] Oikawa R, Takimoto M, Kambayashi Y. Composing Swarm Robot Formations Based on their Distributions Using Mobile Agents, Multi-Agent Systems and Agreement Technologies. EUMAS 2015, Vol. 9571 of Lecture Notes in Computer Science. Springer; 2016. pp. 108-120

[11] Yajima H, Oikawa R, Takimoto M, Kambayashi Y. Practical formation control of swarm robots using Mobile agents. In: Proceedings of the Intelligent Systems Conference. 2017. pp. 1002-1009

[12] Takimoto M, Mizuno M, Kurio M, Kambayashi Y. Saving energy consumption of multi-robots using higher-order mobile agents. In: Proceedings of the First KES International Symposium on Agent and Multi-Agent Systems (KES-AMSTA 2007), Vol. 4496 of Lecture Notes in Artificial Intelligence. Springer-Verlag; 2007. pp. 549-558

[13] Kambayashi Y, Takimoto M. Higher-order mobile agents for controlling intelligent robots. International Journal of Intelligent Information Technologies (IJIIT). 2005;**1**(2):28-42

[14] Kambayashi Y, Ugajin M, Sato O, Tsujimura Y, Yamachi H, Takimoto M, et al. Integrating ant colony clustering to a multi-robot system using mobile agents. Industrial Engineering and Management Systems. 2009;**8**(3):181-193

[15] Dorigo M, Birattari M, Stützle T. Ant colony optimization–artificial ants as a computational intelligence technique. IEEE Computational Intelligence Magazine. 2006;**1**(4):28-39

[16] Dorigo M, Gambardella LM. Ant colony system: A cooperative learning approach to the traveling salesman. IEEE Transactions on Evolutionary Computation. 1996;**1**(1):53-66

[17] Deneubourg J, Goss S, Franks NR, Sendova-Franks AB, Detrain C, Chreien L. The dynamics of collective sorting: Robot-like ant and ant- like robot. In: Proceedings of the First Conference on Simulation of Adaptive Behavior: From Animals to Animats. MIT Press; 1991. pp. 356-363

[18] Wand T, Zhang H. Collective sorting with multi-robot. In: Proceedings of the First IEEE International Conference on Robotics and Biomimetics. 2004. pp. 716-720

[19] Lumer ED, Faiesta B. Diversity and adaptation in populations of clustering ants, from animals to animats 3. In: Proceedings of the 3rd International Conference on the Simulation of Adaptive Behavior. MIT Press; 1994. pp. 501-508

[20] Balch T, Arkin RC. Behavior-based formation control for multirobot teams. Robotics and Automation, IEEE Transactions on. 1998;**14**(6):926-939

[21] Anthony Lewis M, Tan K. High precision formation control of mobile robots using virtual structures. Autonomous Robots. 1997;**4**(4):387-403

[22] Das AK, Fierro R, Kumar V, Ostrowski JP, Spletzer J, Taylor CJ. A vision-based formation control framework. Robotics and Automation, IEEE Transactions on. Oct 2002;**18**(5):813-825

[23] Unsal C, Bay JS. Spatial self-organization in large populations of mobile robots. In: Proceedings of 1994 9th IEEE International Symposium on Intelligent Control. 1994. pp. 249-254

[24] Mamei M, Vasirani M, Zambonelli F. Experiments of morphogenesis in swarms of simple mobile robots. Applied Artificial Intelligence. 2004;**18**(9-10):903-919

[25] Kondacs A. Biologically-inspired self-assembly of two-dimensional shapes using global-to-local compilation. In: Proceedings of the Eighteenth International Joint Conference on Artificial Intelligence; August 9-15, 2003; Acapulco, Mexico. 2003. pp. 633-638

[26] Sty K, Nagpal R. Self-reconfiguration using directed growth. In: Proceedings 7th International Symposium on Distributed Autonomous Robotic Systems. 2004. pp. 1-10

[27] Gordon N, Wagner IA, Bruckstein AM. Discrete bee dance algorithm for pattern formation on a grid. In: 2003 IEEE/WIC International Conference on Intelligent Agent Technology. 2003. pp. 545-549

[28] Rubenstein M, Shen WM. A scalable and distributed approach for self-assembly and self-healing of a differentiated shape. In: 2008 IEEE/RSJ International Conference on Intelligent Robots and Systems. 2008. pp. 1397-1402

[29] Wooldridge M. An Introduction to Multiagent Systems. 2nd ed. Chichester, West Sussex, UK: John Wiley & Son; 2009

[30] Bellifemine F, Caire G, Greenwood D. Developing Multi-Agent Systems with Jade. Chichester, West Sussex, UK: John Wiley & Son; 2007

[31] AgentSpace—A Mobile Agent System. Available from: http://research.nii.ac.jp/~ichiro/

[32] Dorigo M, Gambardella LM. Ant algorithms for discrete optimization. Artificial Life. 1999;**5**(2):137-172

[33] Dorigo M, Stützle T. Ant Colony Optimization. Cambridge, MA, USA: MIT Press; 2004